My Giant

Sticker

Puzzle Book

1

Tough Trucks

Jigsaw truck

Which puzzle piece completes the picture?

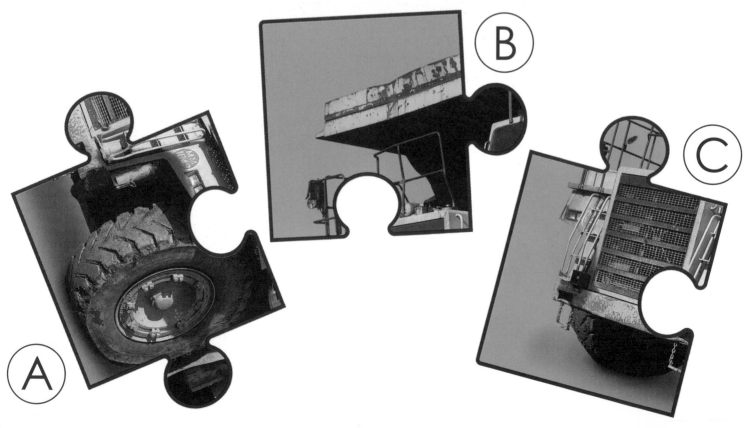

Follow the lines

Trace over the lines to take the workers to their trucks.

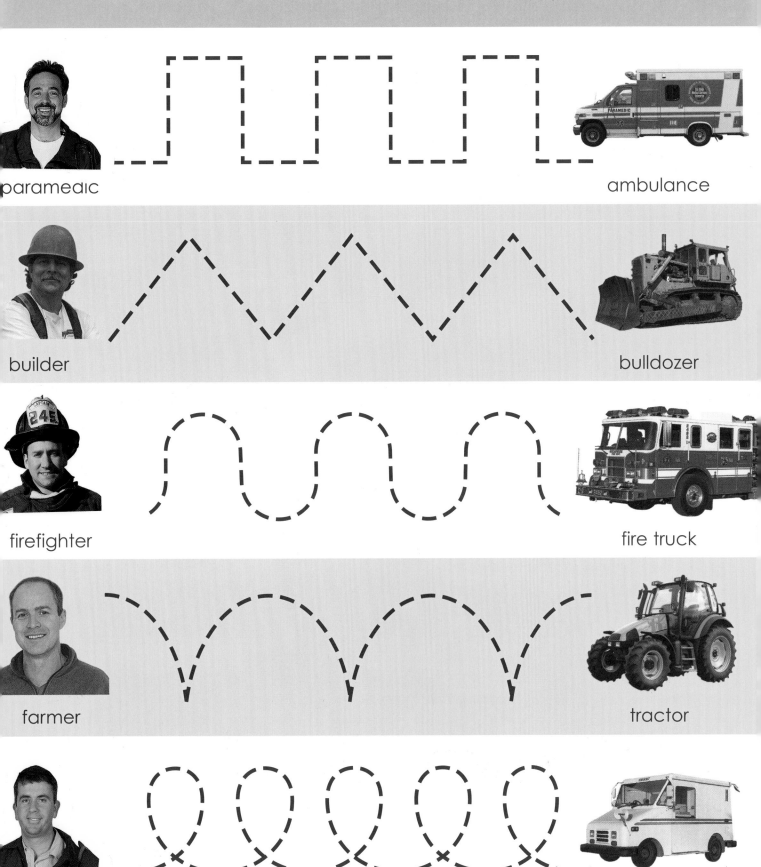

paramedic

ambulance

builder

bulldozer

firefighter

fire truck

farmer

tractor

mailman

mail truck

Counting trucks

Count the amount of each type of truck,
then write the numbers in the boxes.

How many
diggers can
you count?

How many big
rigs can you
count?

How many fire trucks can you count?

How many tractors can you count?

How many dump trucks can you count?

How many pickups can you count?

Find and match

Find the stickers, then color in the pictures that match.

school bus

fire truck

Learn to draw

delivery truck

look

delivery truck

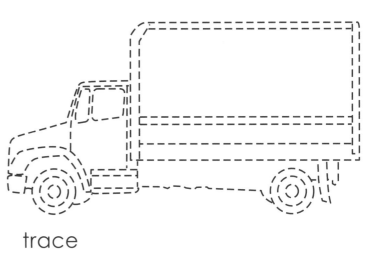

trace

Now draw the truck and write its name.

d_____ _____

Linking lines

Draw a line between each truck and the color it matches.

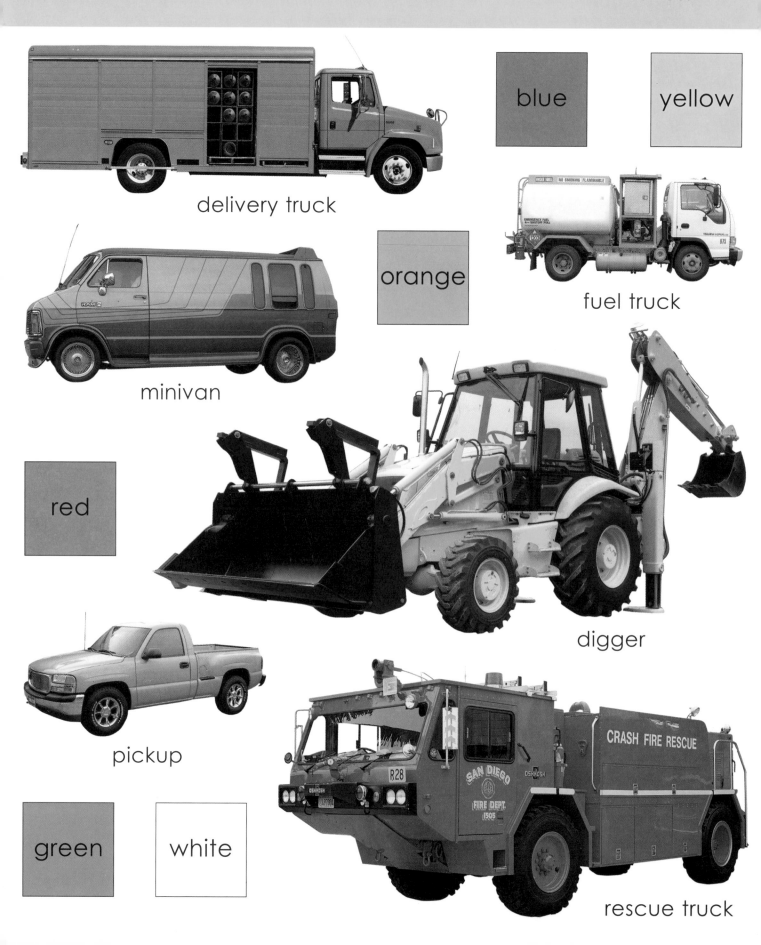

delivery truck

blue

yellow

orange

fuel truck

minivan

red

digger

pickup

green

white

rescue truck

Adding trucks

Write the number of trucks in the boxes, then add them up.

Matching trucks

Draw lines between the pairs of matching trucks.

Find and match

Find the stickers, then circle the pair of white trucks and the pair of yellow trucks.

transporter

6

water truck

scraper

tipper truck

delivery truck

school bus

giant excavator

repair truck

Drawing trucks

Look at the picture and the words, then trace over the outlines.

fire truck

look

fire truck

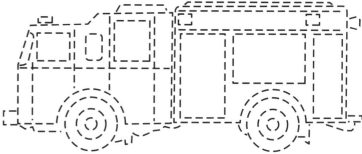

trace

Now draw the truck and write its name.

f_____ _____

How many?

Count the trucks, then write each number in the boxes.

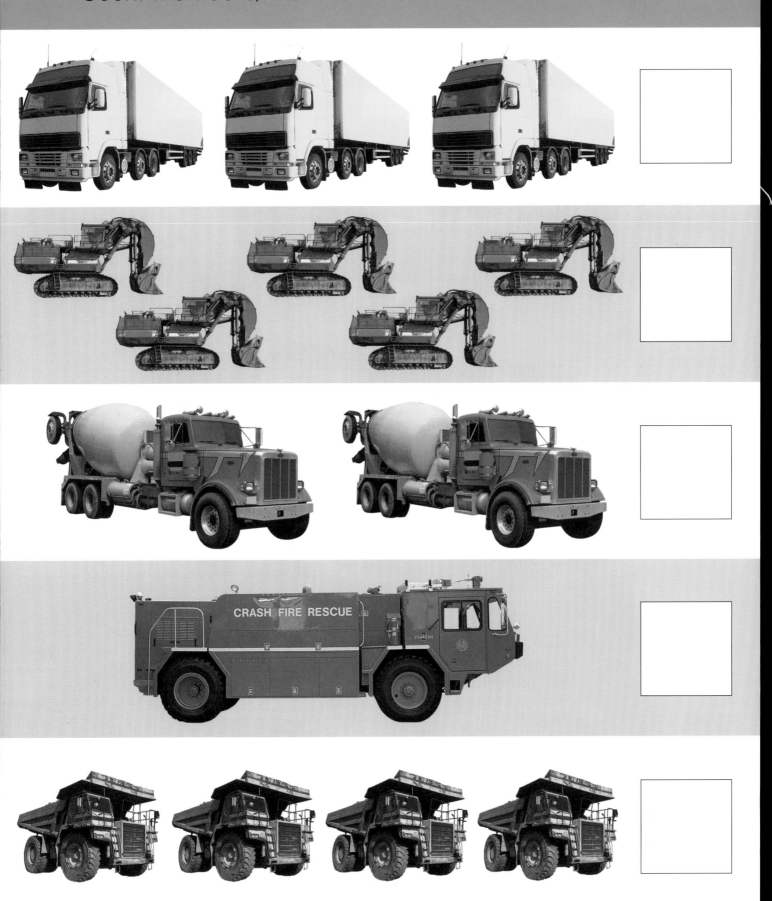

Sticker search

Can you find the stickers of the other fire trucks?

fire truck

Dot to dot

Join the dots to draw the picture, then color it in
using the colored dots as a guide.

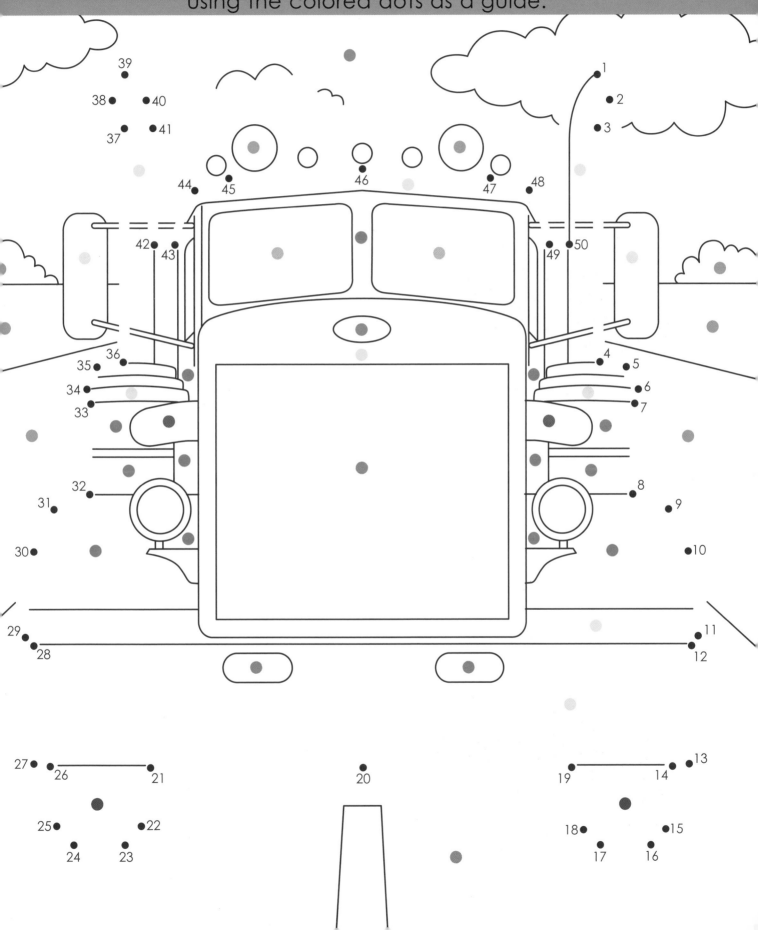

What's different?

Can you find six differences between these two pictures?
Circle the differences on picture B when you find them.

Mixer maze

Find a way through the maze that takes the driver
to the cement mixer.

start

finish

Counting trucks

Sort the trucks into colors, then write the number of each in the boxes.

How many red trucks can you count?

How many blue trucks can you count?

How many white
trucks can
you count?

How many yellow
trucks can
you count?

How many green trucks
can you
count?

How many black trucks
can you
count?

Drawing trucks

Look at the picture and the word, then trace over the outlines.

dump truck

look

dump truck

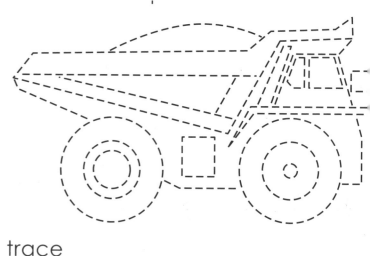

trace

Now draw the truck and write its name.

d_____ _____

Missing letters

Trace over the missing letters to complete the truck names.

 tr**u**ck

 di**g**ger

 min**i**va**n**

 b**u**lldo**z**er

What's different?

There are six differences between these two pictures.
Circle the differences on picture B when you find them.

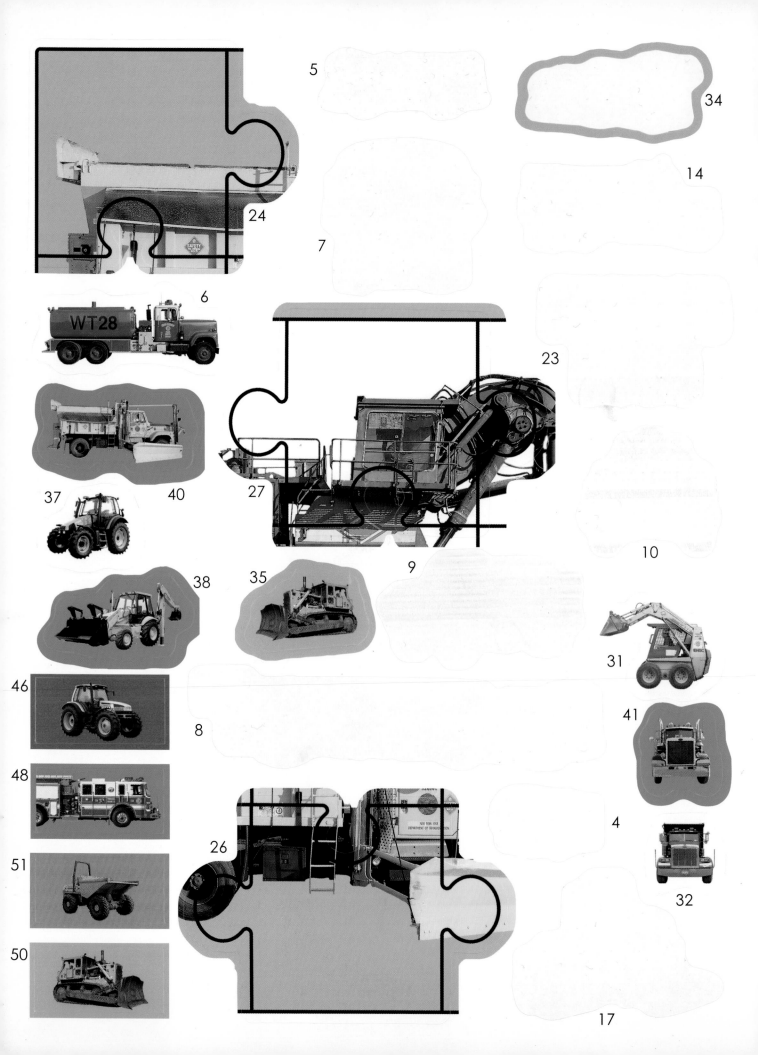

5

34

14

24

7

6

WT28

23

37 40

27

38 35

9

10

46 31

8

48 41

51 4

26

50 32

17

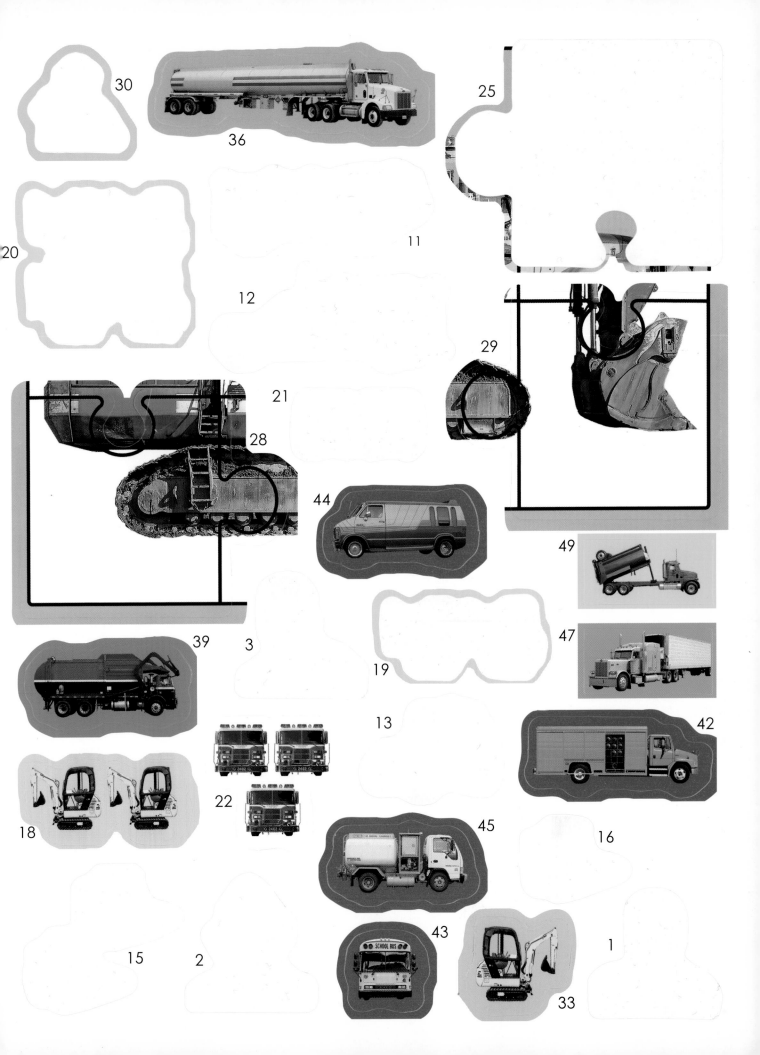

30

36

25

20

11

12

29

21

28

44

49

39

3

47

19

18

22

13

42

45

16

15

2

43

33

1

Police trail

Which trail will take the police officer to her car?

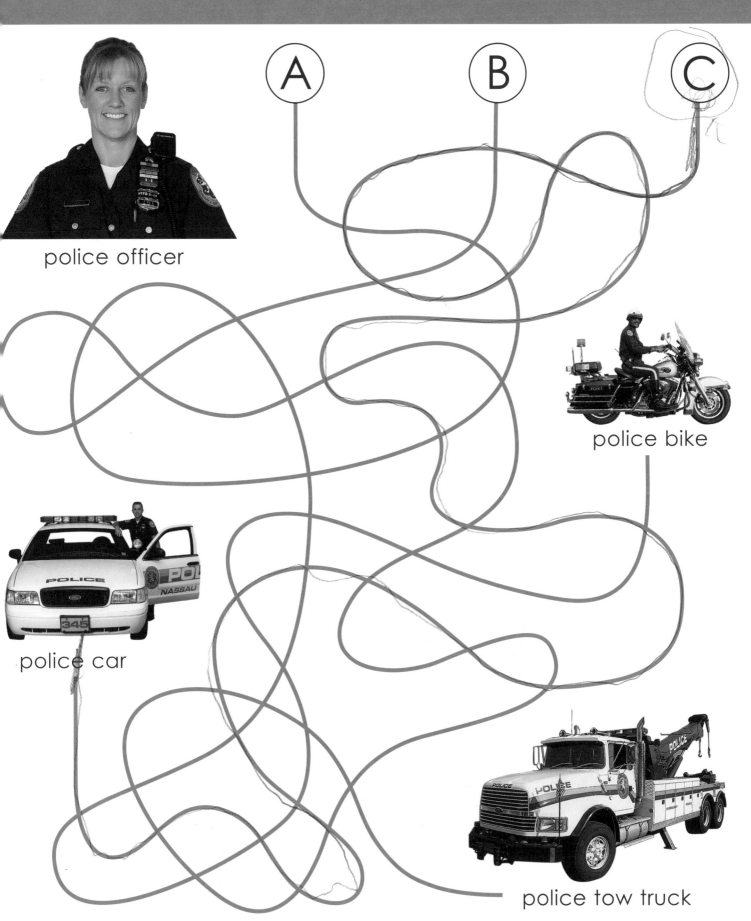

police officer

police bike

police car

police tow truck

Letter link

Draw a line between each truck and the letter
its name begins with.

pickup

a

f

tractor

dump truck

p

bulldozer

ambulance

t

d

b

fire truck

Learn to draw

Look at the picture and the word, then trace over the outlines.

digger

look

digger

trace

Now draw the truck and write its name.

d _ _ _ _ _ _

Busy trucks

Use your pens to color in this truck picture.

Writing practice

Trace over the outlines to write the words below.

firefighter

bus

fuel tanker

tractor

Learn to draw

Look at the picture and the word, then trace over the outlines.

bulldozer

look

bulldozer

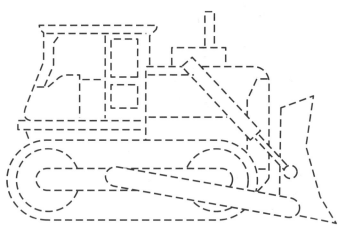

trace

Now draw the truck and write its name.

b_____

Emergency maze

Find a way through the maze for the paramedic to reach the ambulance.

start

finish

What's different?

Which one of these pictures does not belong with the others?

firefighter

fire chief's truck

fire truck

helicopter pilot

Missing halves

Find the stickers, then draw the other halves of the pictures.

tractor

tipper truck

Adding truck

Find the stickers, write the numbers of trucks in the boxes, then add them up.

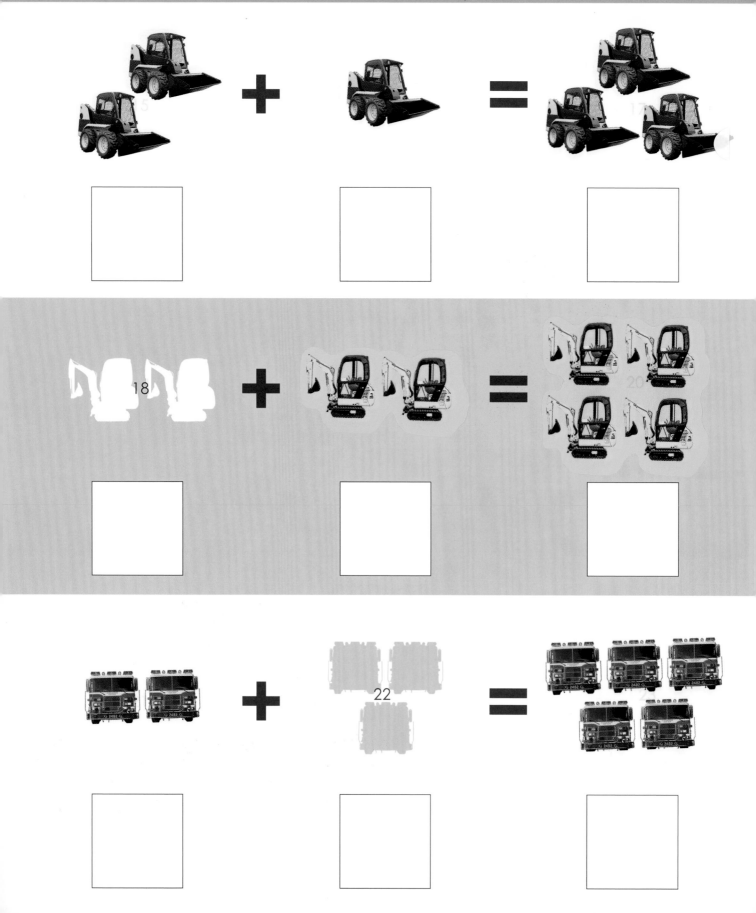

Jigsaw puzzle

Find the missing jigsaw stickers to complete the pictures.

24

25

26

snow plow

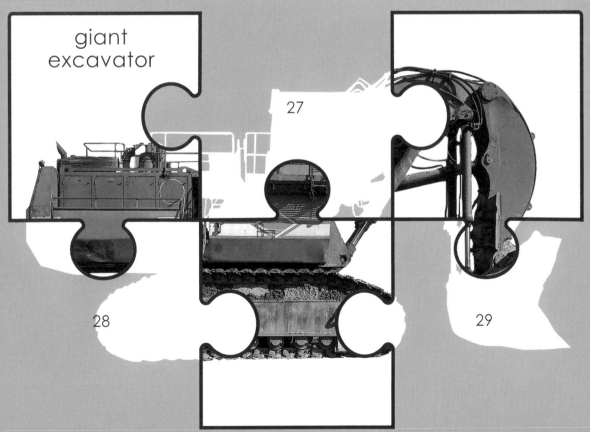

giant excavator

27

28

29

Find and match

Find the stickers, then color in the pictures that match.

construction worker

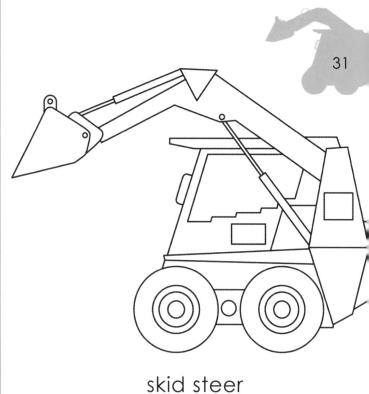

skid steer

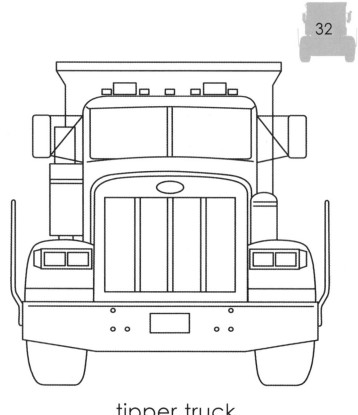

tipper truck

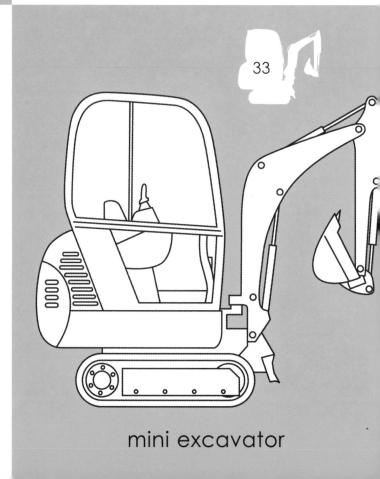

mini excavator

Truck names

Trace over the outlines to write the truck names.

big rig

dump truck

tractor

bus

Dot to dot

Join the dots to draw the pictures, then color them in
using the colored dots as a guide.

tractor

firefighter

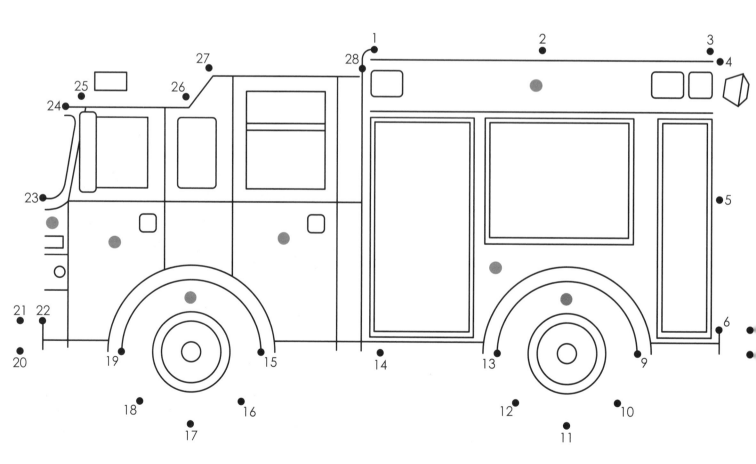

fire truck

Exactly the same

Only two of these trucks are exactly the same.
Can you tell which ones?

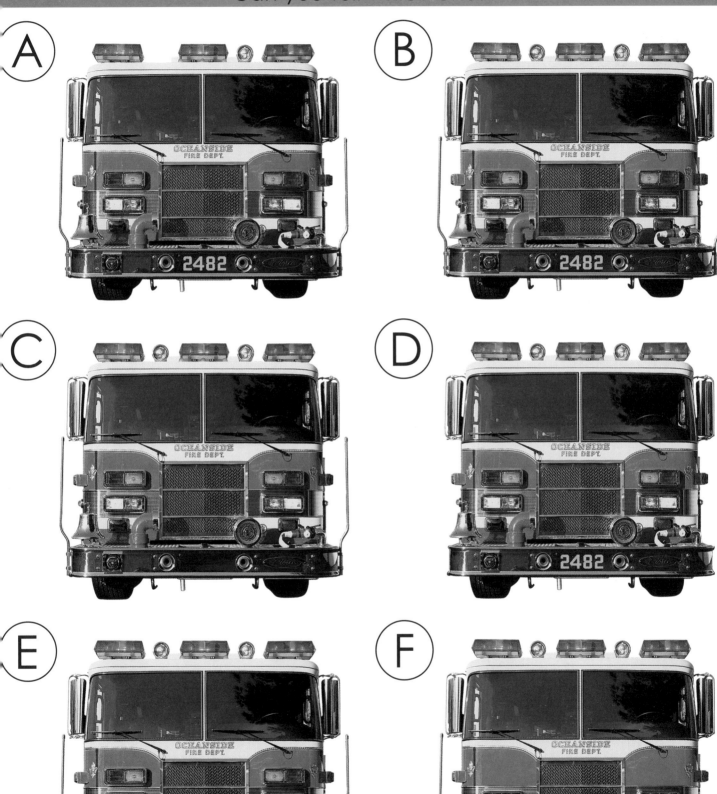

Number practice

Trace over the outlines to practice writing numbers and find the stickers that fit on the opposite page.

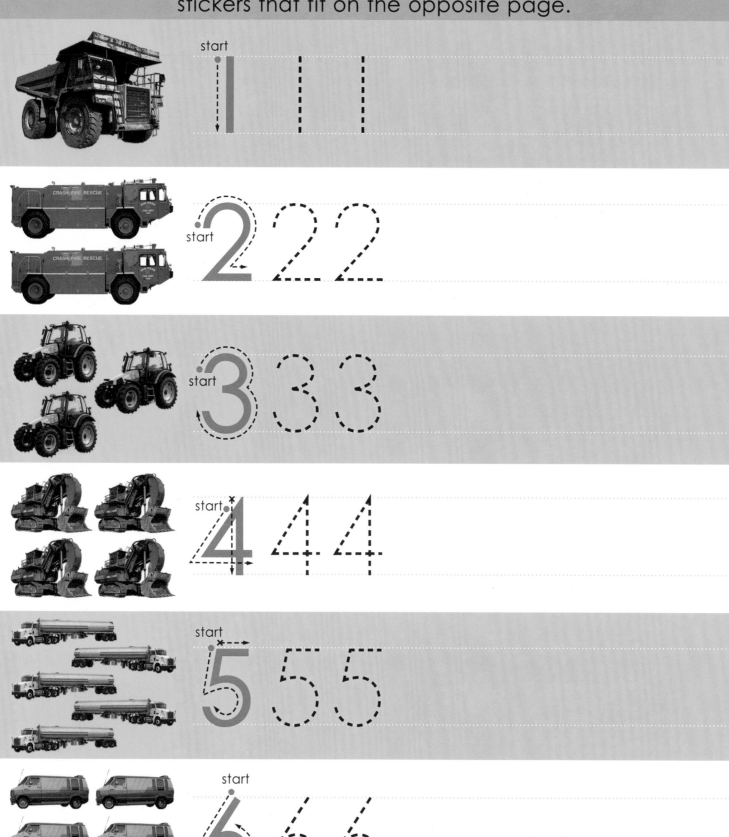

start
1 1 1

start
2 2 2

start
3 3 3

start
4 4 4

start
5 5 5

start
6 6 6

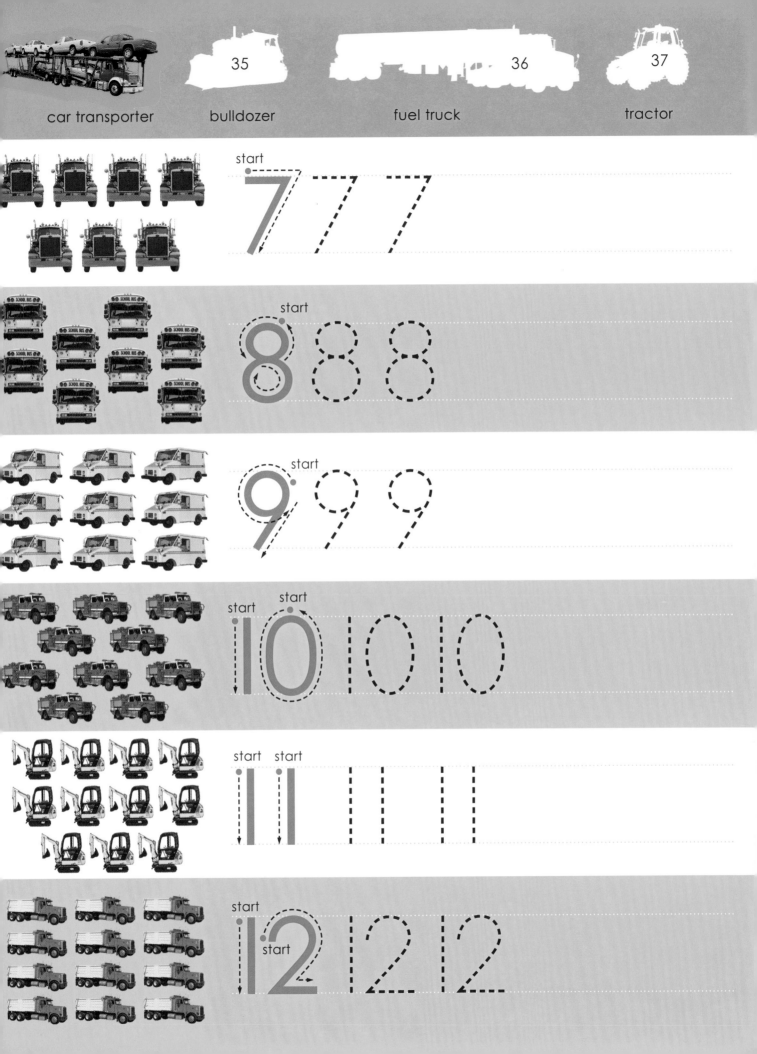

car transporter

bulldozer
35

fuel truck
36

tractor
37

start
7 7 7

start
8 8 8

start
9 9 9

start start
10 10 10

start start
11 I I I

start
start
12 12 12

Letter practice

Trace over the outlines to practice writing letters and find the stickers that fit on the opposite page.

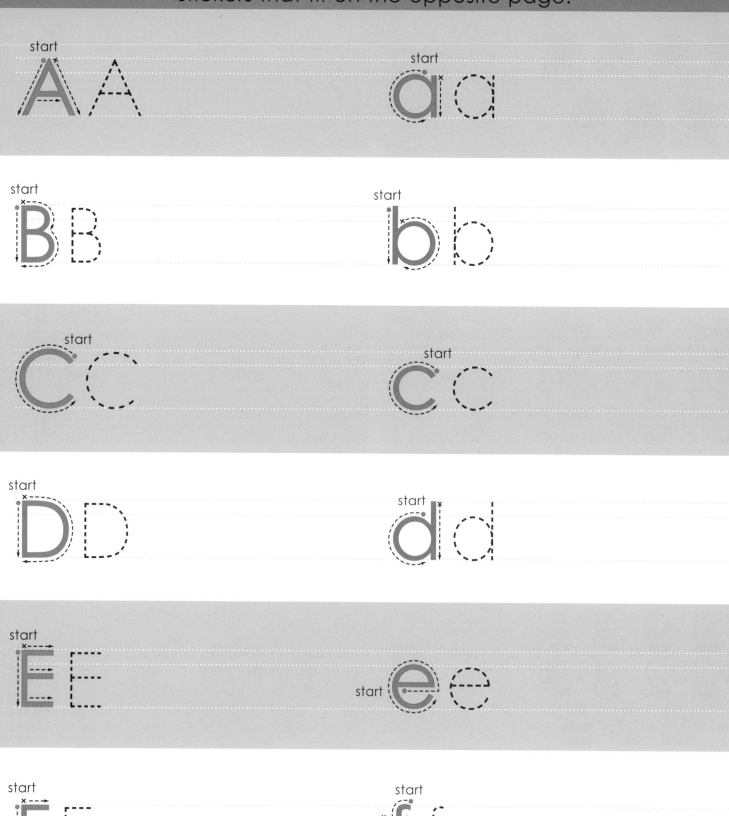

38	39	40	41
digger	garbage truck	snow plow	big rig

start
G G

start
g g

start
H H

start
h h

start
I I

start
i i

start
J J

start
j j

start
K K

start
k k

start
L L

start
l l

Letter practice

Trace over the outlines to practice writing letters and find the stickers that fit on the opposite page.

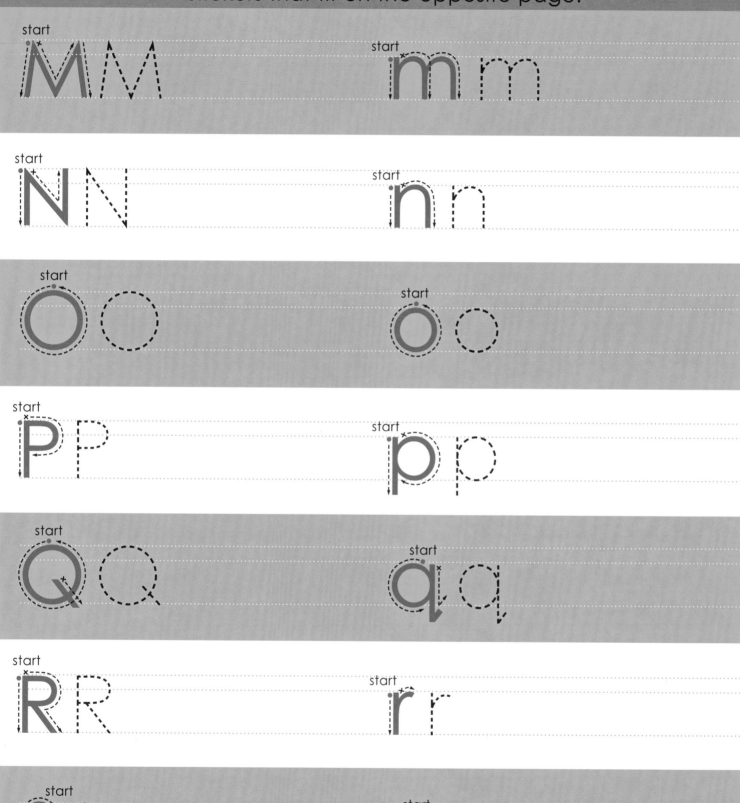

start
M M M

start
m m m

start
N N N

start
n n n

start
O O O

start
o o o

start
P P P

start
p p p

start
Q Q Q

start
q q q

start
R R R

start
r r r

start
S S S

start
s s s

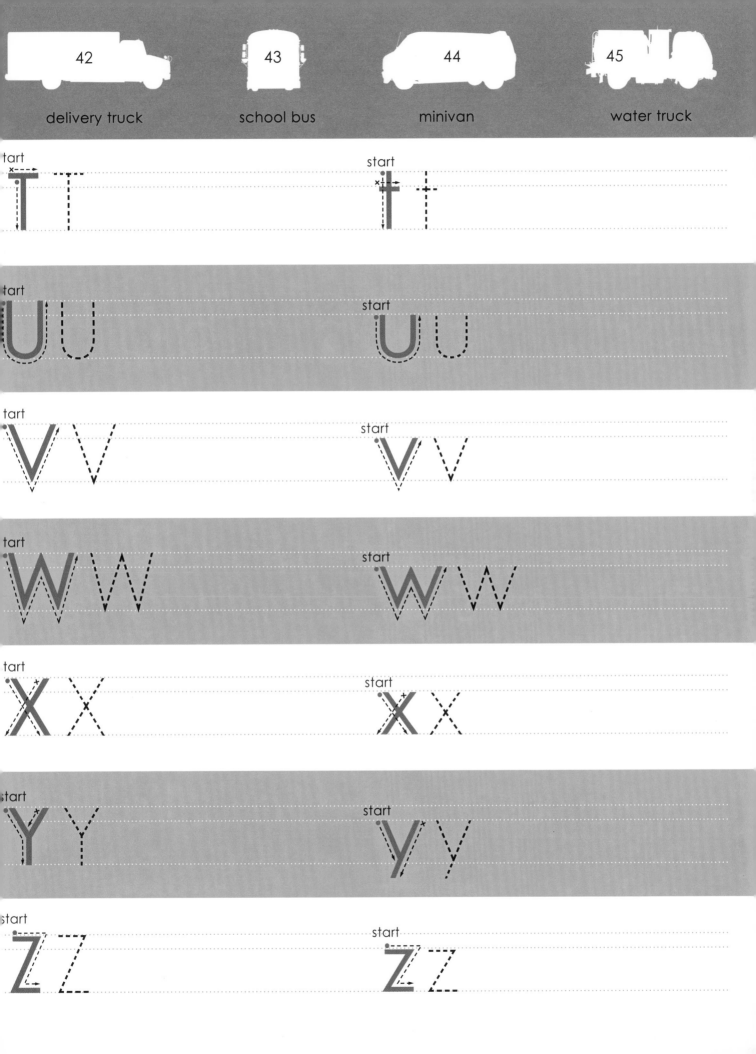

42	43	44	45
delivery truck	school bus	minivan	water truck

start
Tt

start
Tt

start
Uu

start
Uu

start
Vv

start
Vv

start
Ww

start
Ww

start
Xx

start
Xx

start
Yy

start
Yy

start
Zz

start
Zz

Word search

Find the stickers, then look for the words in the box.

f	i	r	e	t	r	u	c	k	d
h	q	t	j	a	i	u	j	k	u
g	s	r	u	x	s	t	b	h	m
b	p	a	f	u	b	l	i	c	p
w	h	c	v	i	e	c	g	b	t
t	r	t	i	p	p	e	r	m	r
i	h	o	s	e	f	t	i	j	u
p	k	r	n	c	z	b	g	m	c
b	v	o	e	c	n	r	i	v	k
j	b	u	l	l	d	o	z	e	r

 46 tractor

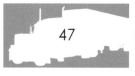 47 big rig

 48 fire truck

 49 tipper

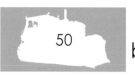 50 bulldozer

 51 dump truck

My Giant Sticker Puzzle Book

1

Busy Bugs

Picture problem

Which jigsaw piece completes the picture?

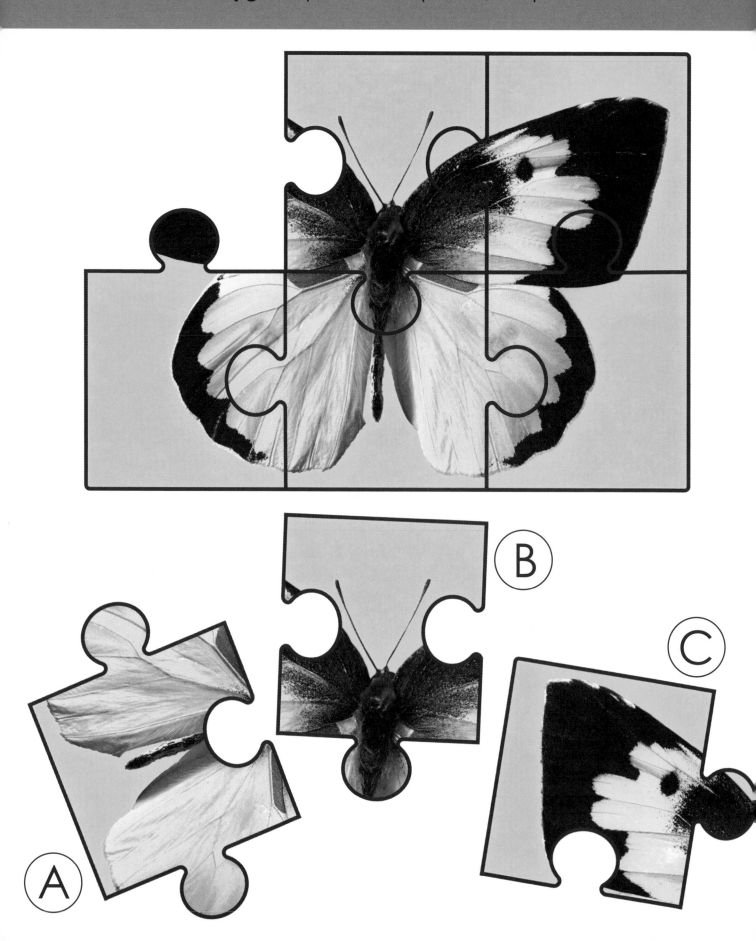

Follow the lines

Use your pen to trace over the lines between the bugs.

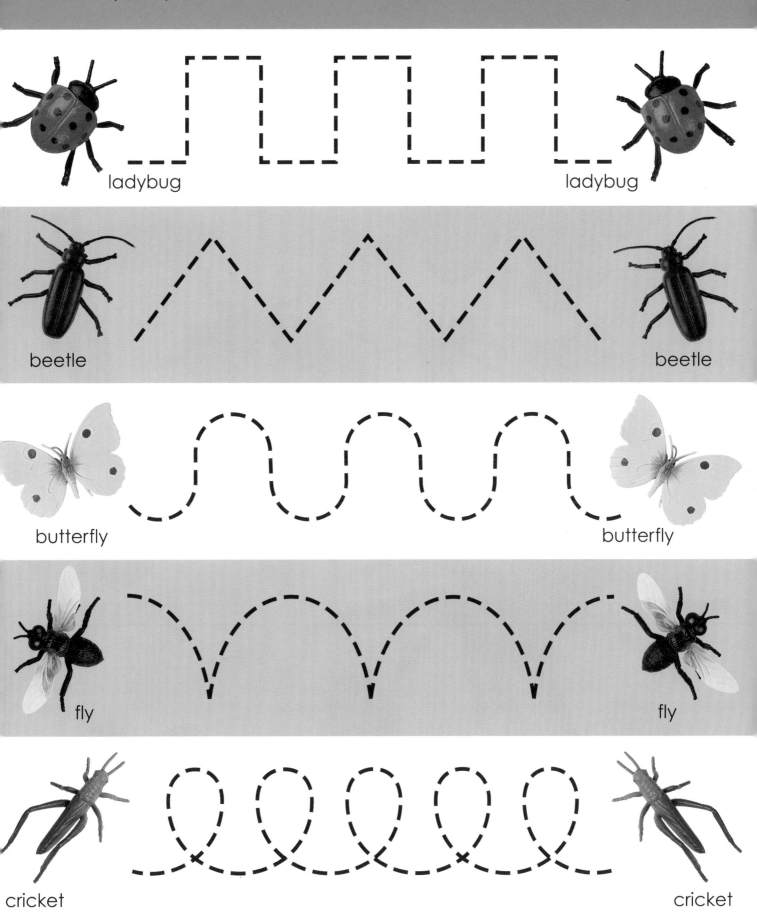

ladybug   ladybug

beetle   beetle

butterfly   butterfly

fly   fly

cricket   cricket

Counting bugs

Count the bugs and little critters and write the numbers of each in the boxes.

How many praying mantids can you count?

How many snails can you count?

How many
butterflies can
you count?

How many
ladybugs can
you count?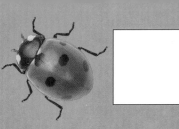

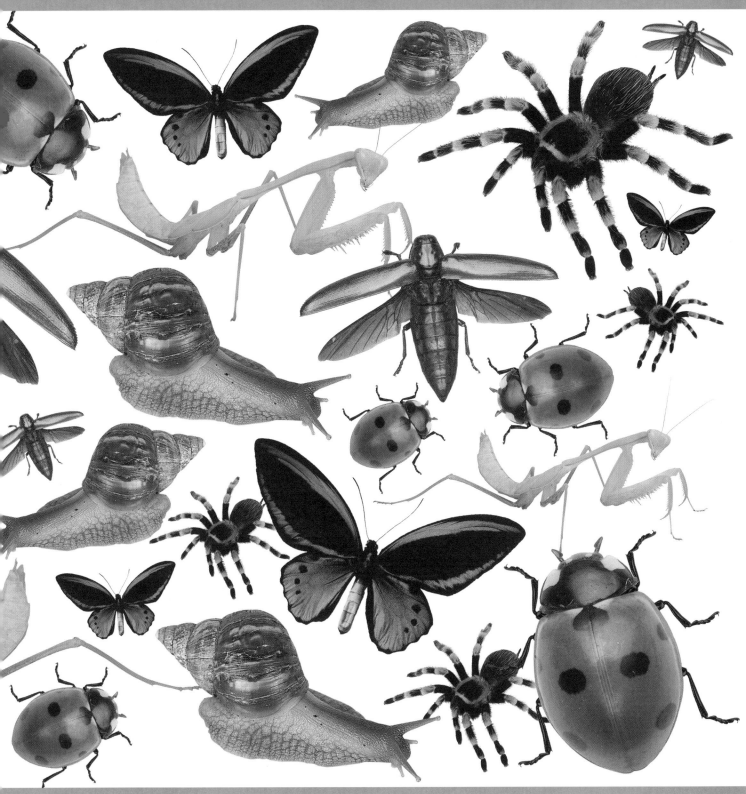

How many
beetles can
you count?

How many
spiders can
you count?

Bug pictures

Find the bug stickers, then color in the pictures.

dragonfly

52

beetle

53

Drawing bugs

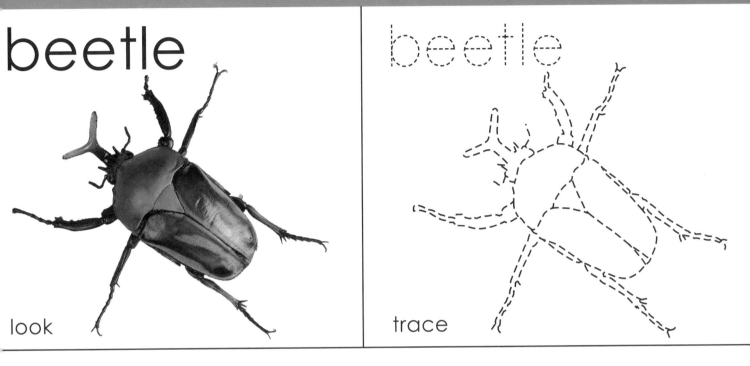

beetle

look

beetle

trace

Now draw the beetle and write the word.

b _ _ _ _ _

Matching letters

Draw a line between each creature and the letter
its name begins with.

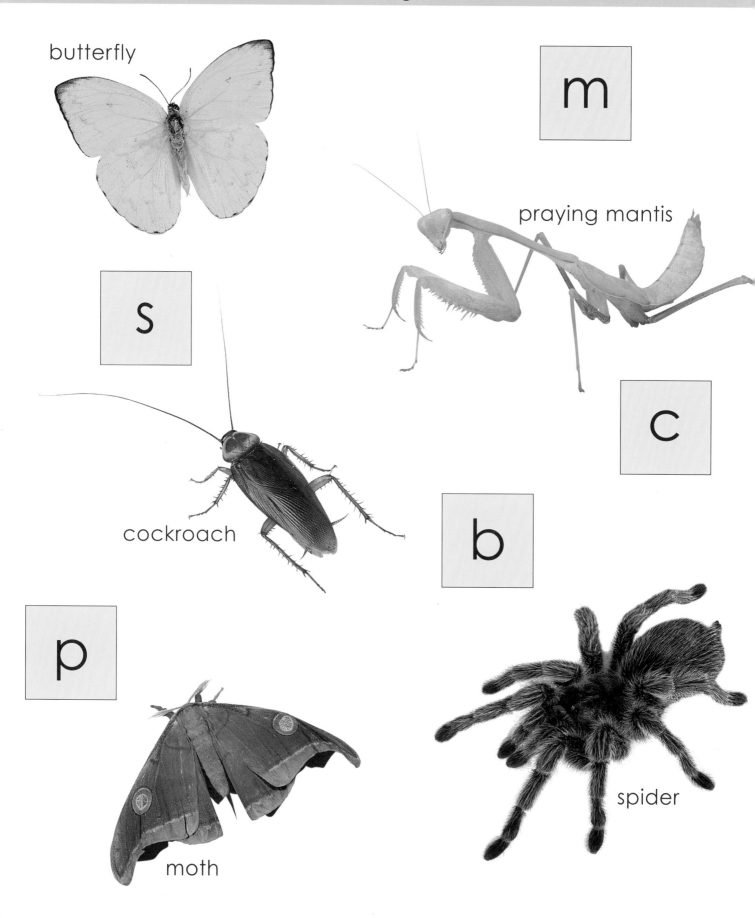

butterfly

m

praying mantis

s

c

cockroach

b

p

moth

spider

Adding bugs

Write the numbers of bugs in the boxes, then add them together.

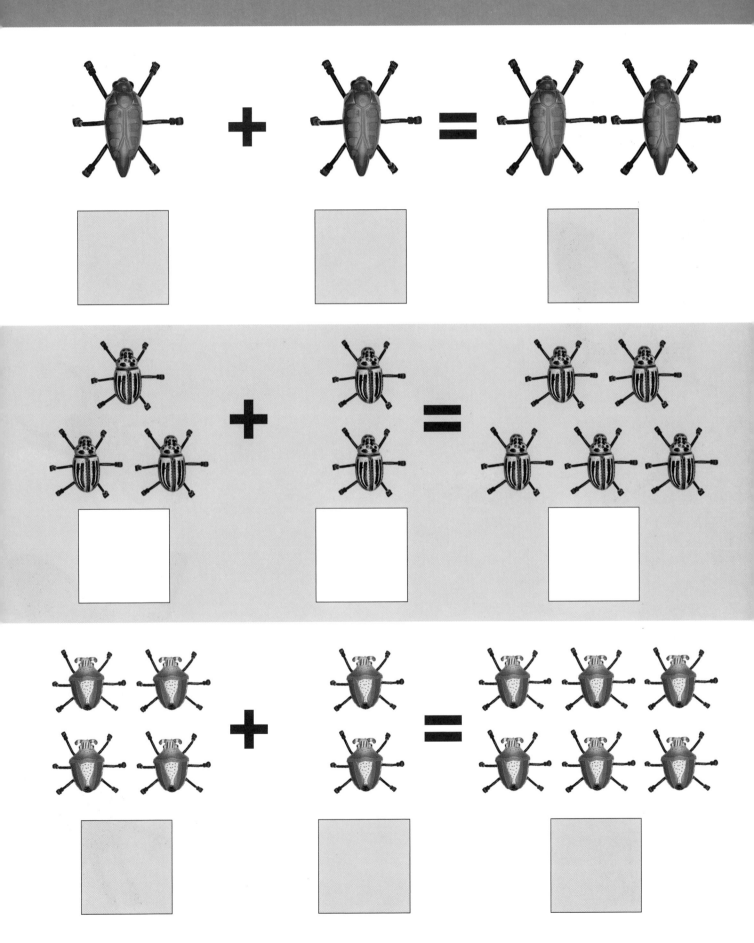

Mix and match

Draw lines between the matching pairs of creatures.

54

55

Who's missing?

Which of the bugs in picture A is missing from picture B?

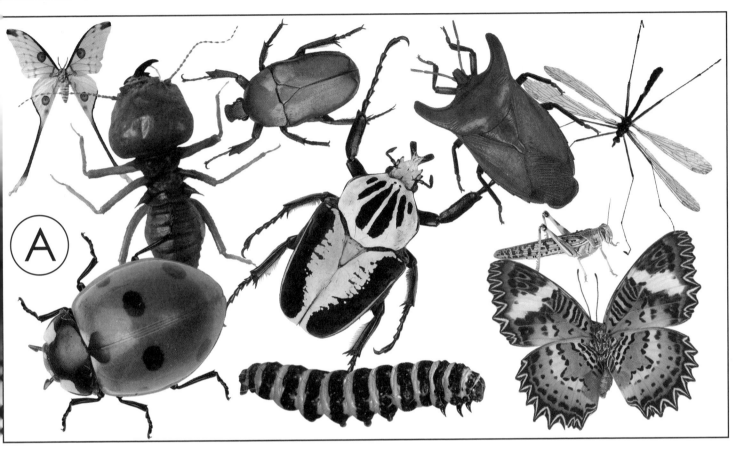

Drawing butterflies

Look at the picture and the word, then trace the outlines.

butterfly

look

butterfly

trace

Now draw the butterfly and write the word.

b _ _ _ _ _ _ _ _

How many?

Count the bugs and write each number in the boxes.

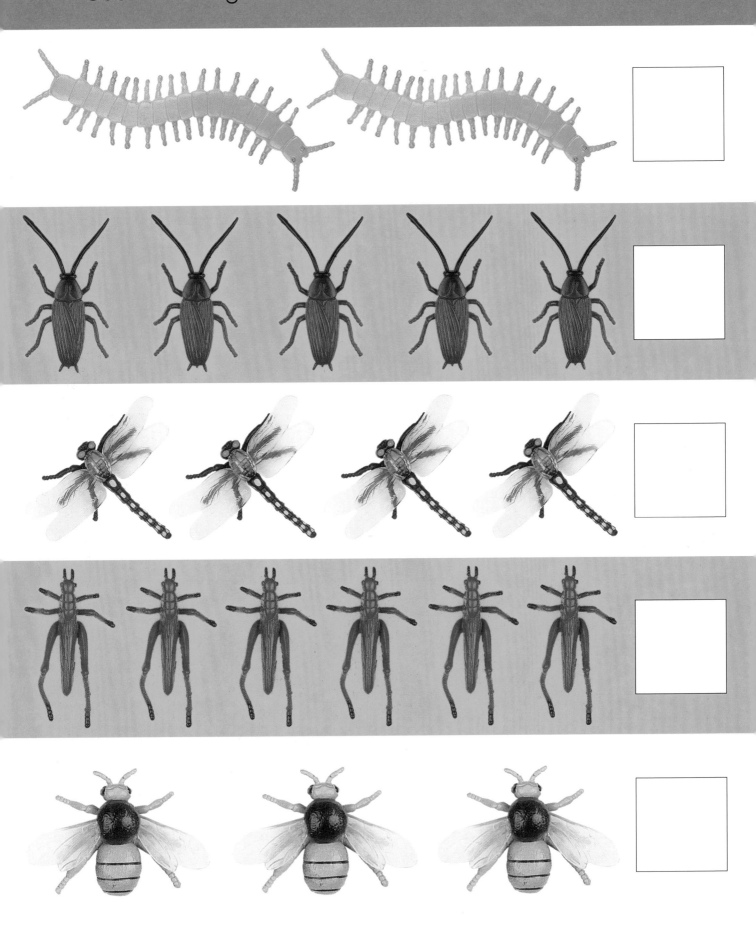

Find the stickers

Find the butterfly stickers that fit the spaces below.
Which one matches the picture?

Dot to dot

Join the dots to complete the bug pictures, then color them in using the colored dots as a guide.

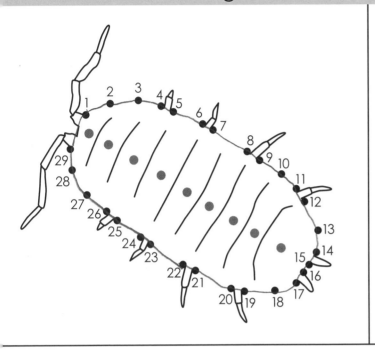

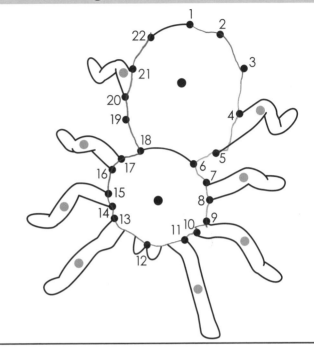

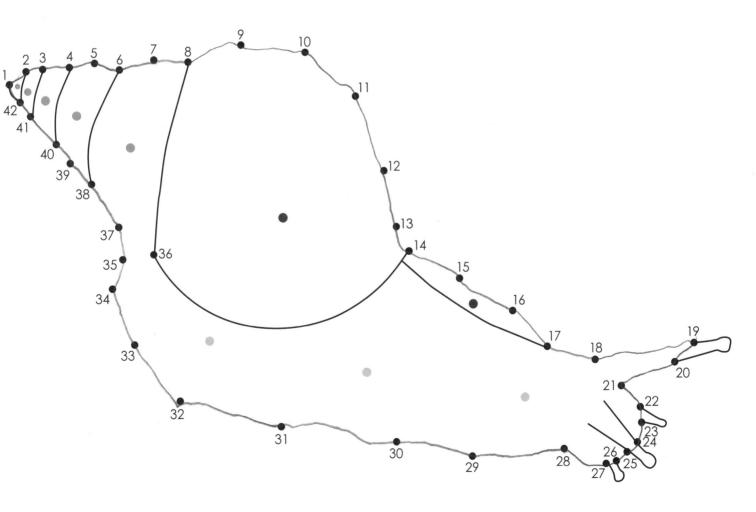

What's different?

There are six differences between these two pictures.
Circle each difference on picture B when you spot them.

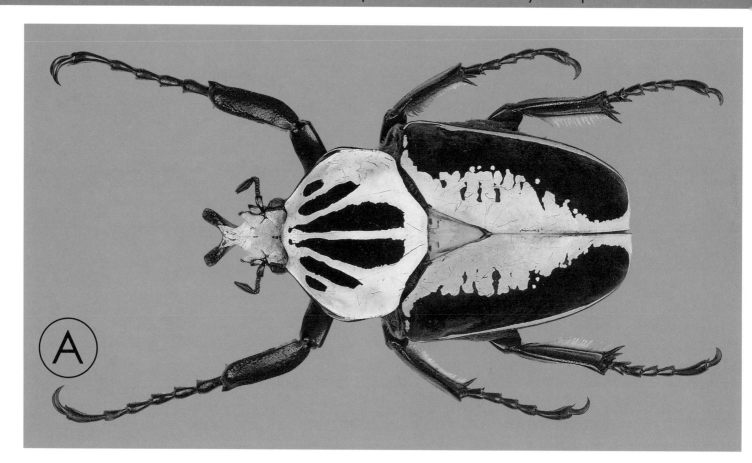

A

B

Sunflower maze

Find a way through the maze that takes the bee to the sunflower.

start

finish

Butterfly count

Write the number of each color of butterfly in the boxes.

How many
white butterflies
can you count? 4

How many
yellow butterflies
can you count?

Drawing spiders

Look at the picture and word, then trace the outlines.

spider

look

spider

trace

Now draw the spider and write its name.

s _____

Missing letters

Trace over the letter outlines to complete the words.

 moth

 beetle

 ant

butterfly

What's different?

There are six differences between these two pictures.
Circle the differences on picture B when you find them.

A

B

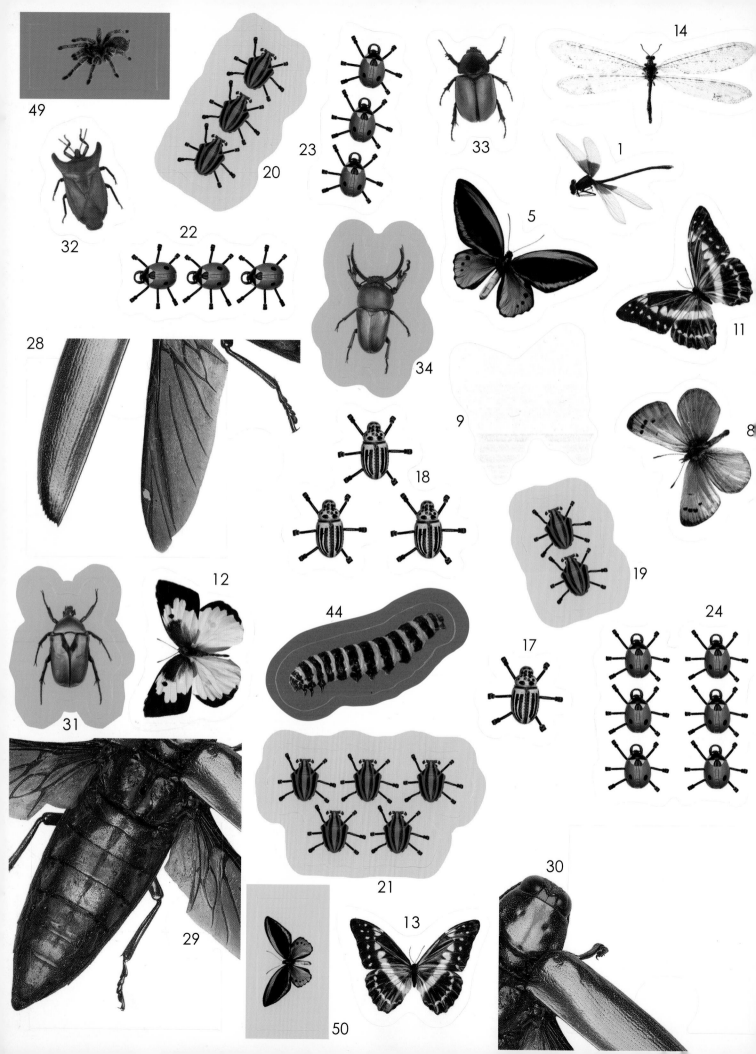

51

35

45

48

6

39

16

26

40

27

4

2

42

7

3

38

25

15

36

10

41

43

47

37

46

52

Butterfly trail

Which trail takes the small butterfly to the big one?

Scorpion scene

Use your pens or pencils to color in this scorpion picture.

Drawing dragonflies

Look at the picture and the word, then trace the outlines.

dragonfly

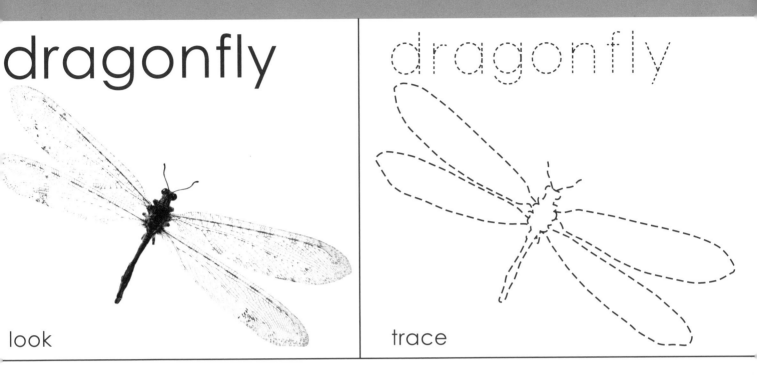

look

dragonfly

trace

Now draw the dragonfly and write its name.

d_ _ _ _ _ _ _ _

In the garden

Use your pens or pencils to color in this bug scene.

Writing practice

Trace over the letters of the bug names below.

praying mantis

praying mantis

scorpion

scorpion

spider

spider

caterpillar

caterpillar

Drawing snails

Look at the picture and word, then trace the outlines.

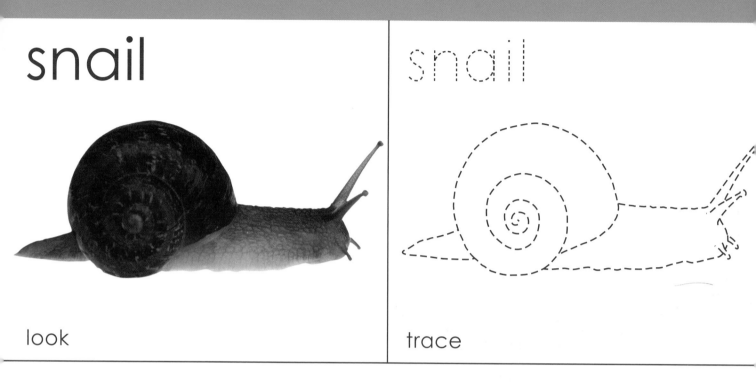

snail

look

snail

trace

Now draw the snail and write its name.

s _ _ _ _ _

Ant maze

Can you find a way through the maze for the
ant to reach the other ants?

start

finish

What's different?

Which one of these creatures is different from the others?

Missing halves

Find the stickers, then draw the other halves of the bugs.

butterfly

dragonfly

Adding bugs

Find the stickers, write the numbers of bugs in the boxes,
then add them together.

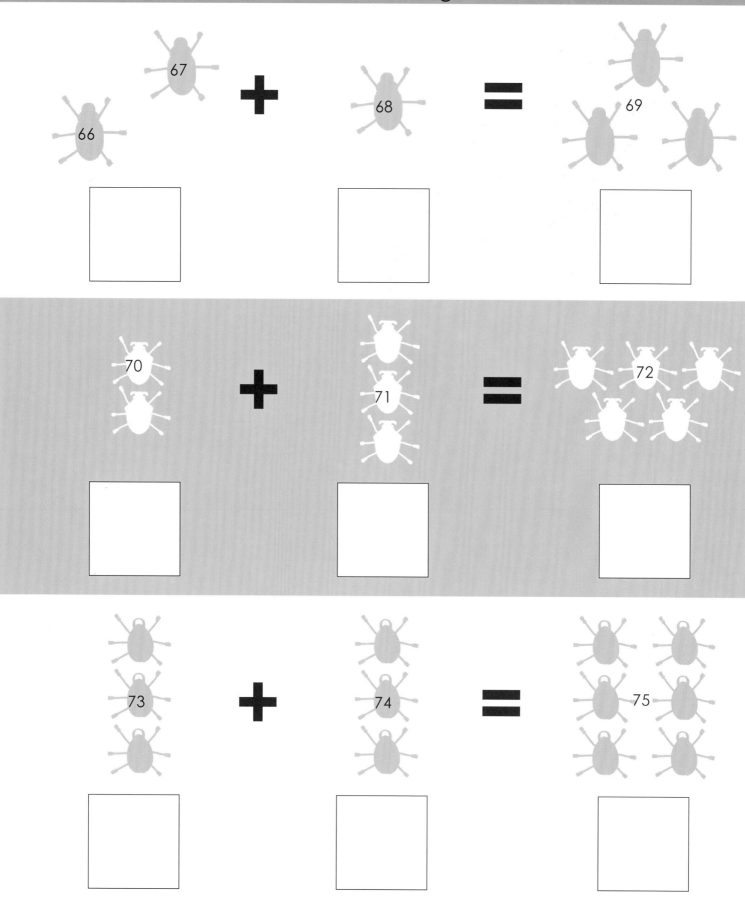

Jigsaw puzzle

Find the jigsaw stickers that complete the pictures below.

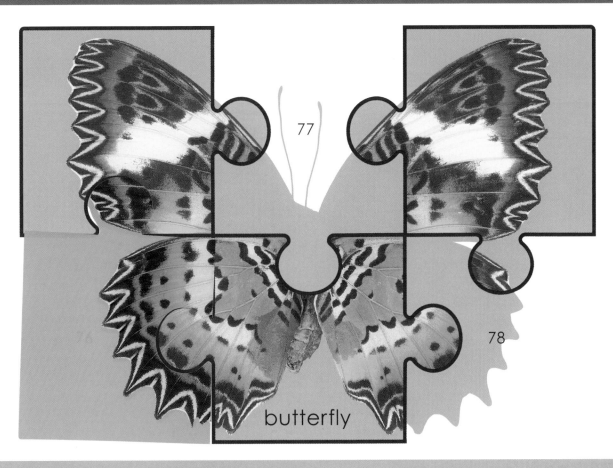

77

78

butterfly

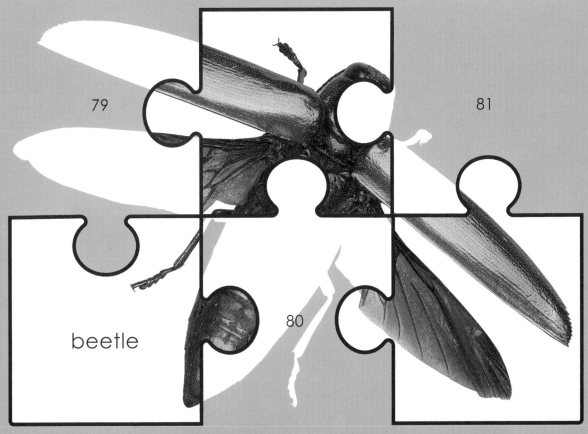

79

81

80

beetle

Bug pictures

Find the stickers, then color in the pictures that match.

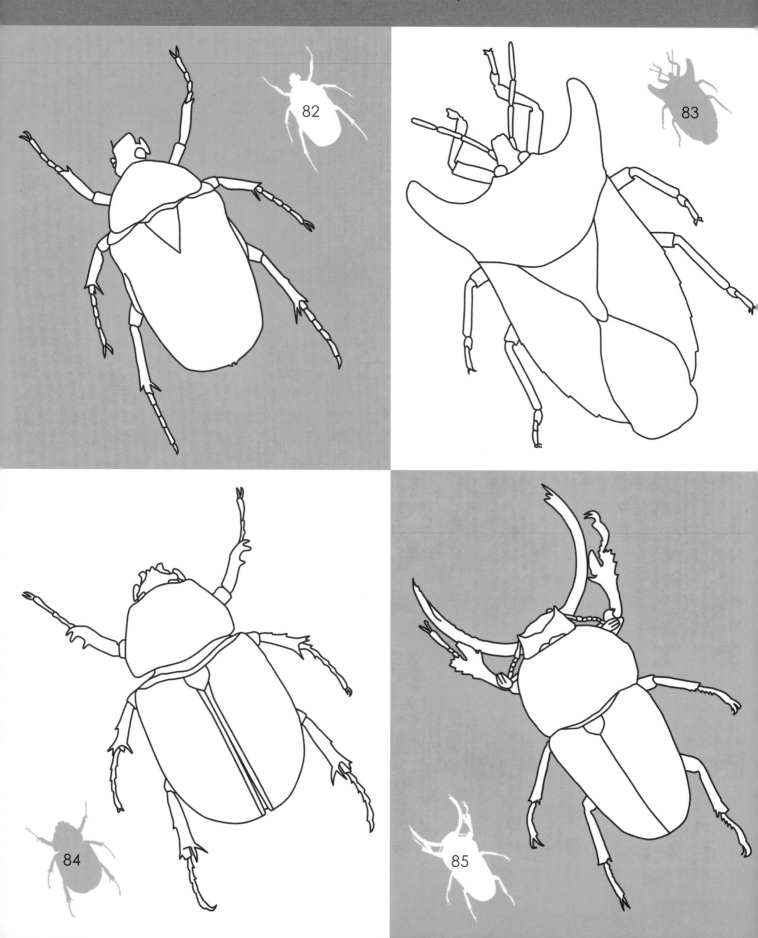

82

83

84

85

Bug words

Trace over the letters of the bug words below.

wings

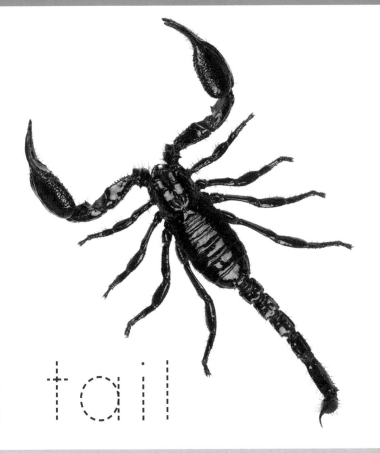

tail

horns

legs

Dot to dot

Join the dots to complete these bug pictures, then color them in using the colored dots as a guide.

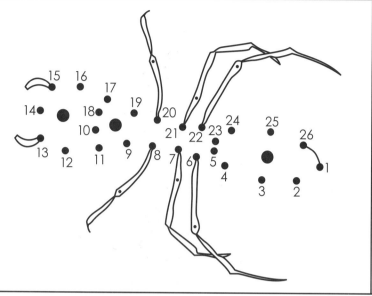

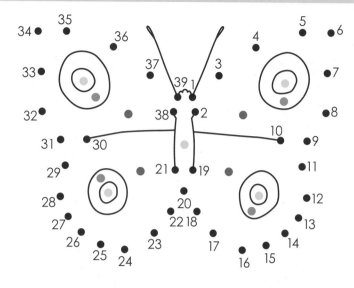

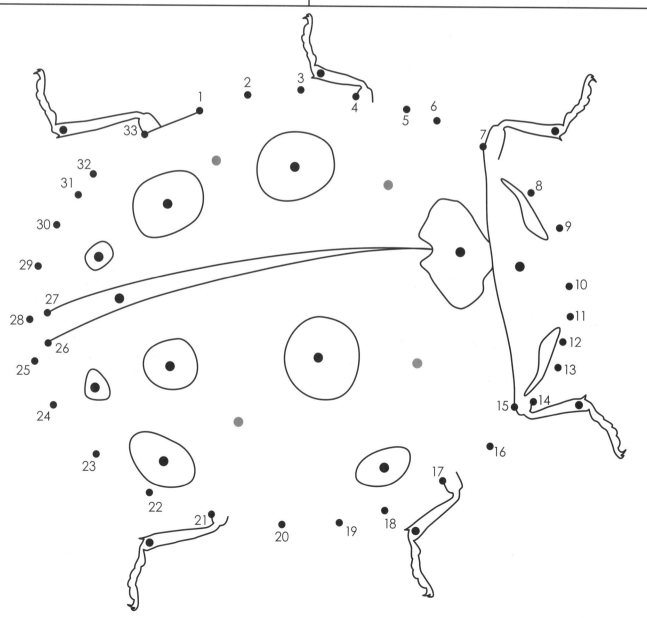

Exactly the same

Only two of these butterflies are exactly the same.
Look closely to find them.

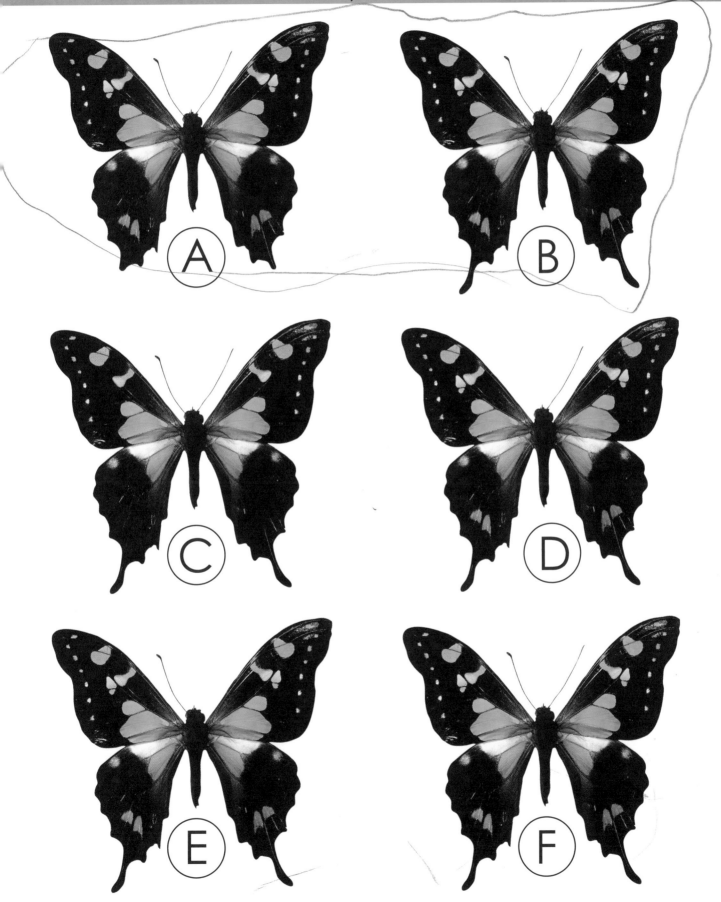

Number practice

Trace the outlines to practice writing numbers and find the stickers that fit on the opposite page.

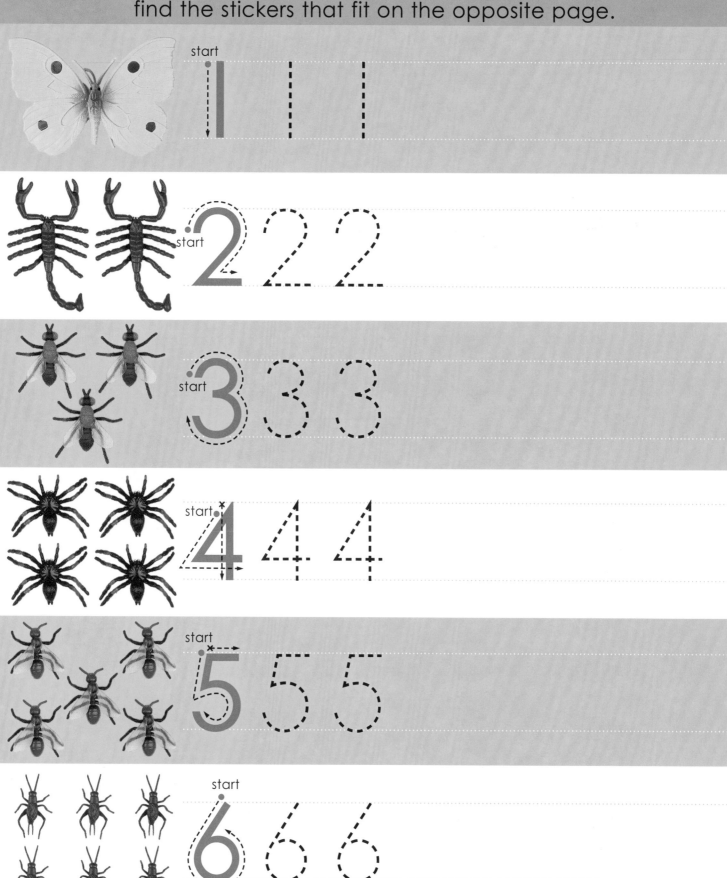

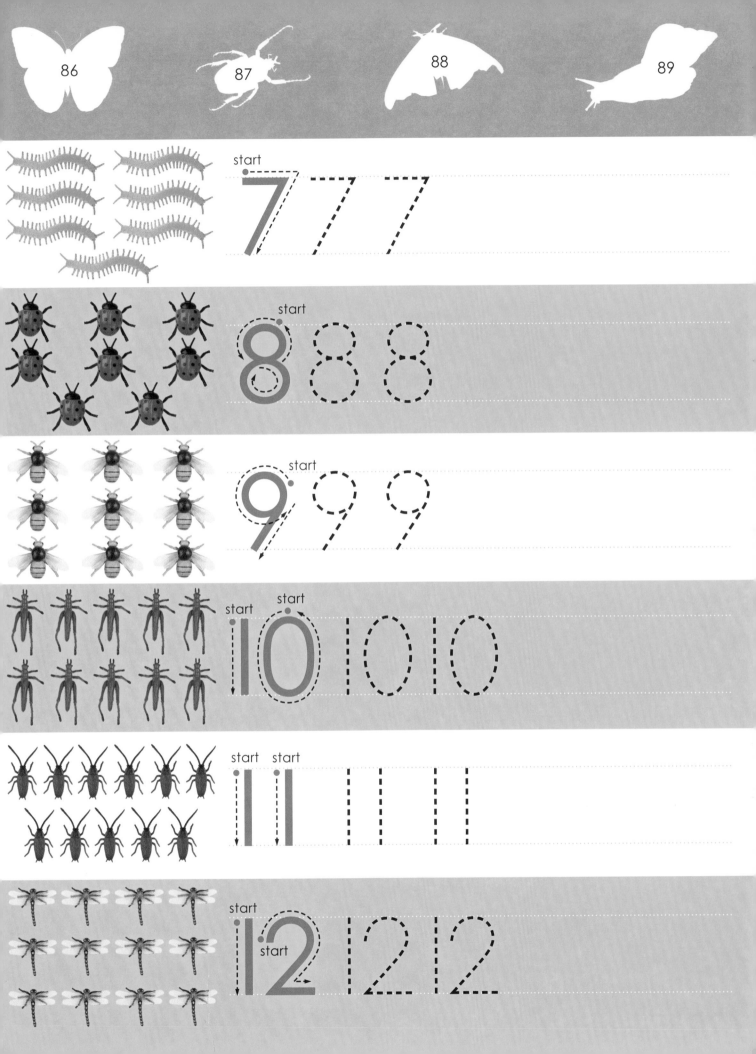

86   87   88   89

start
7 7 7 7

start
8 8 8

start
9 9 9

start start
10 10 10

start start
1 1 1 1 1 1

start
start
12 12 12

Letter practice

Trace the outlines to practice writing letters and find the stickers that fit on the opposite page.

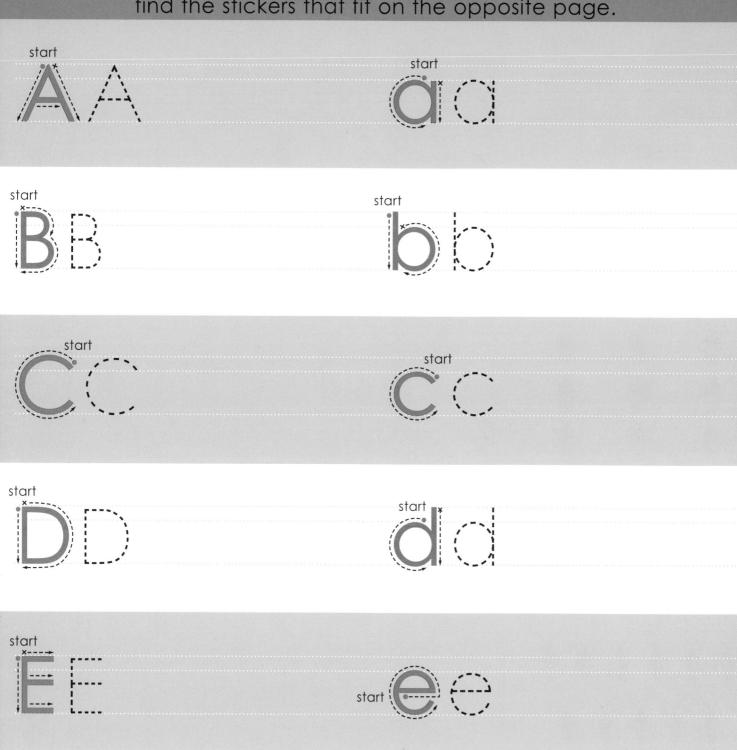

start A A

start a a

start B B

start b b

start C C

start c c

start D D

start d d

start E E

start e e

start F F

start f f

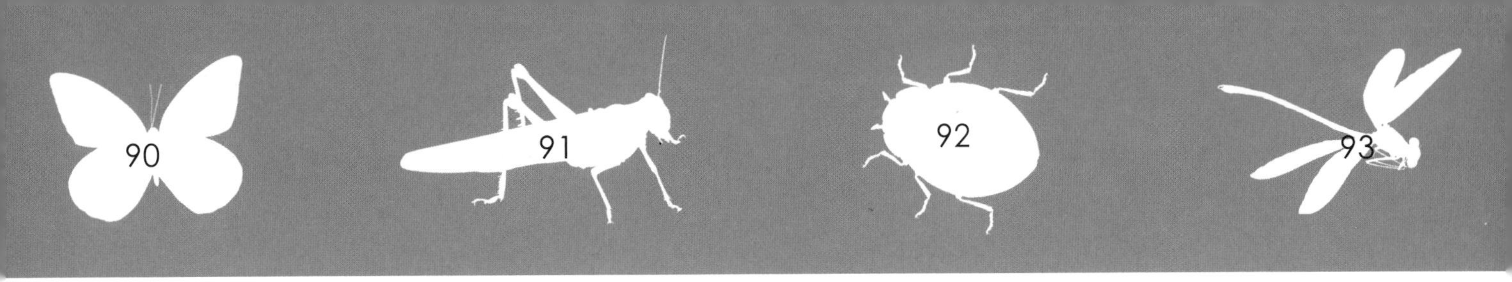

start
G G

start
g g

start
H H

start
h h

start
I I

start
i i

start
J J

start
j j

start
K K

start
k k

start
L L

start
l l

Letter practice

Trace the outlines to practice writing letters and find the stickers that fit on the opposite page.

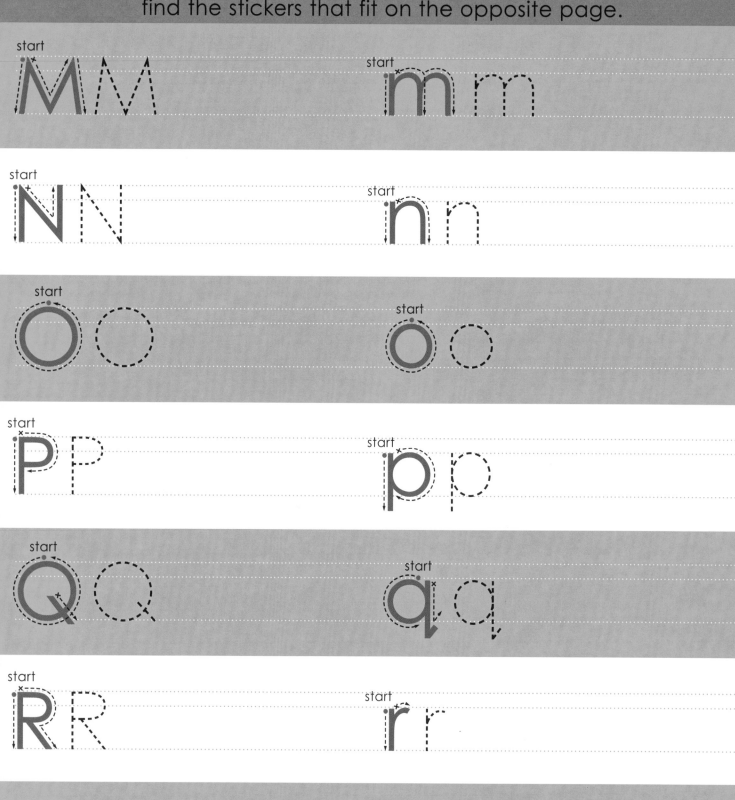

start
M M
start
m m

start
N N
start
n n

start
O O
start
o o

start
P P
start
p p

start
Q Q
start
q q

start
R R
start
r r

start
S S
start
s s

start
T T

start
t t

start
U U

start
U U

start
V V

start
V V

start
W W

start
W W

start
X X

start
X X

start
Y Y

start
Y y

start
Z Z

start
Z z

Word search

Find the stickers, then look for the words in the box.

b	u	t	t	e	r	f	l	y	e
a	y	s	a	a	m	k	t	a	a
r	e	x	n	e	i	d	r	n	r
e	h	e	t	a	o	r	z	c	w
s	w	o	i	o	i	x	l	c	i
p	i	u	m	t	e	l	i	o	g
i	y	l	s	r	e	m	t	u	b
d	a	e	x	r	m	h	o	r	r
e	q	e	t	h	u	e	n	t	m
r	c	z	s	l	i	s	a	m	h

 98 snail

 99 earwig

 100 spider

 101 butterfly

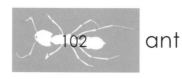 102 ant

 103 moth

My Giant Sticker Puzzle Book

1

Dinosaurs

Picture problem

Which jigsaw piece completes the picture?

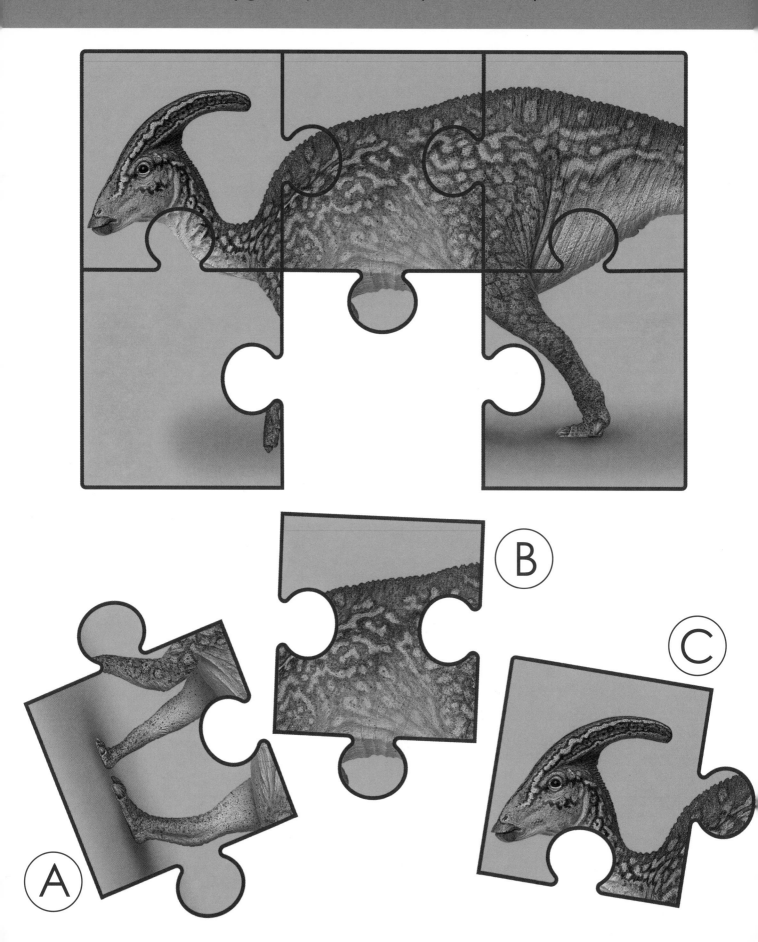

A

B

C

Follow the lines

Use your pen to trace over the lines between the dinosaurs.

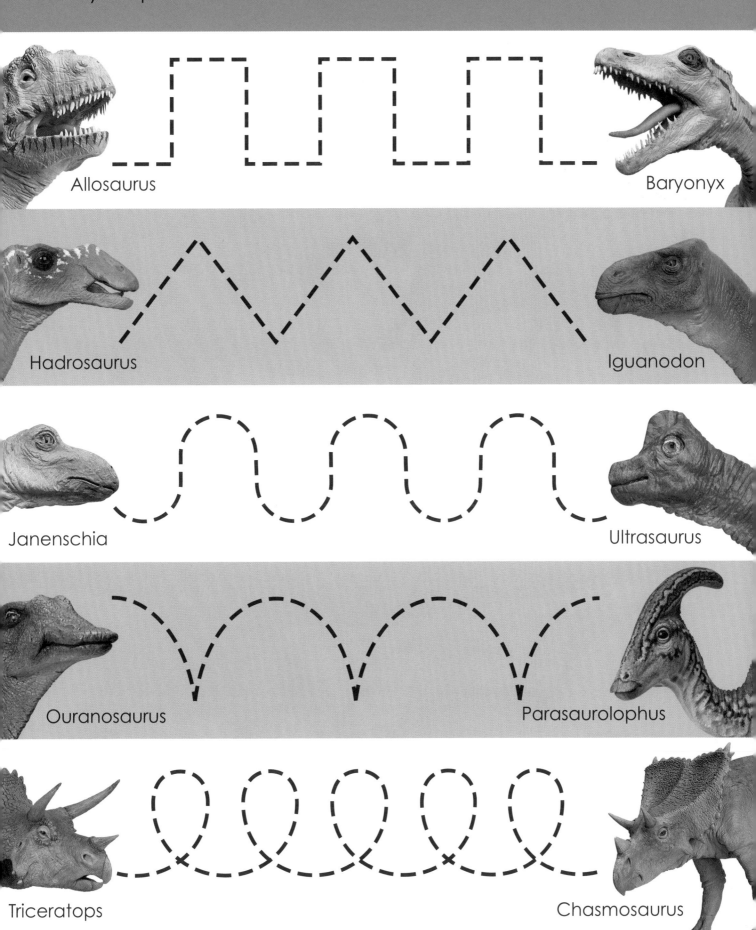

Allosaurus

Baryonyx

Hadrosaurus

Iguanodon

Janenschia

Ultrasaurus

Ouranosaurus

Parasaurolophus

Triceratops

Chasmosaurus

Counting dinosaurs

Count the dinosaurs and write the numbers of each in the boxes.

How many pictures
of Diplodocus
are there?

How many pictures
of Coelophysis
are there?

How many pictures
of Kentrosaurus
are there?

How many pictures
of Triceratops
are there?

How many pictures
of Euoplocephalus
are there?

How many pictures
of Allosaurus
are there?

Prehistoric pictures

Find the dinosaur stickers, then color in the scenes.

104

Riojasaurus

105

Hadrosaurus

Drawing dinosaurs

Look at the picture and dinosaur name, then trace the outlines.

Tyrannosaurus rex

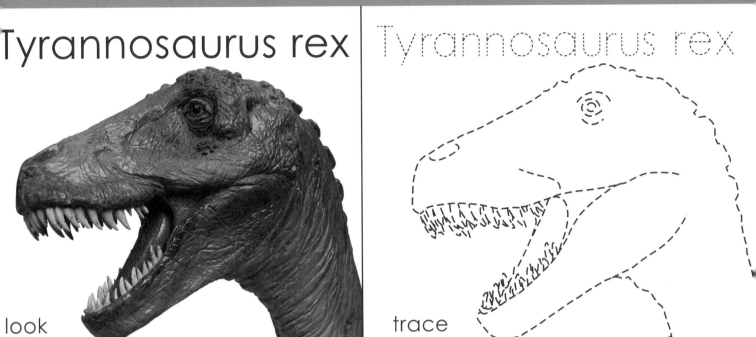

look

trace

Now draw the dinosaur and write its name.

Matching letters

Draw a line between each dinosaur and the letter its name begins with.

Baryonyx

V

S

Stenonychosaurus

U

Velociraptor

B

L

Leptoceratops

Ultrasaurus

Adding dinosaurs

Write the numbers of dinosaurs in the boxes,
then add them together.

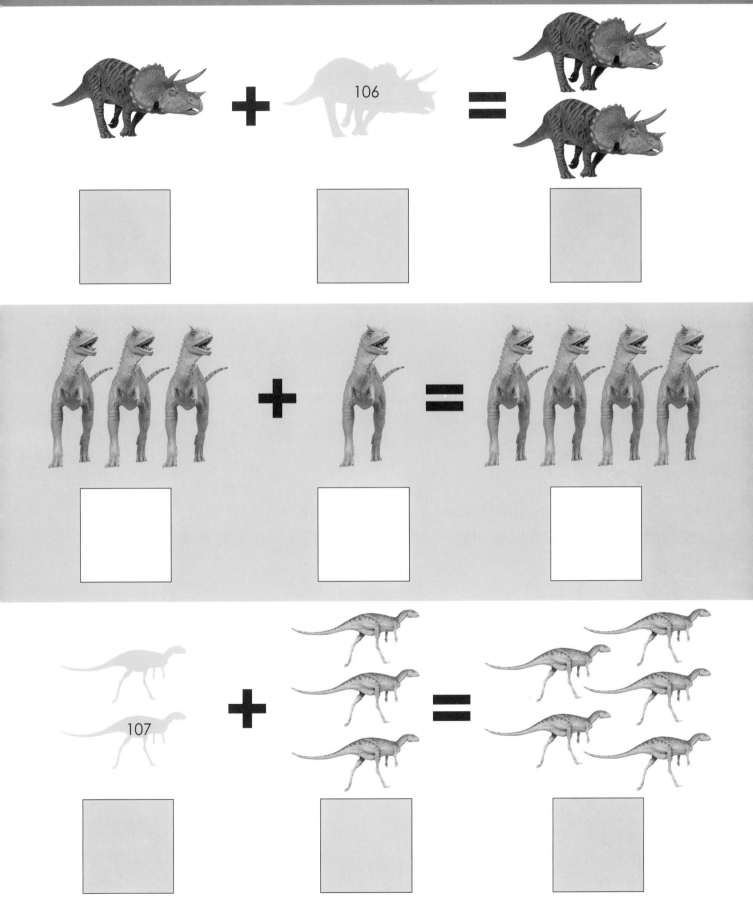

Mix and match

Draw lines between the matching pairs of dinosaurs.

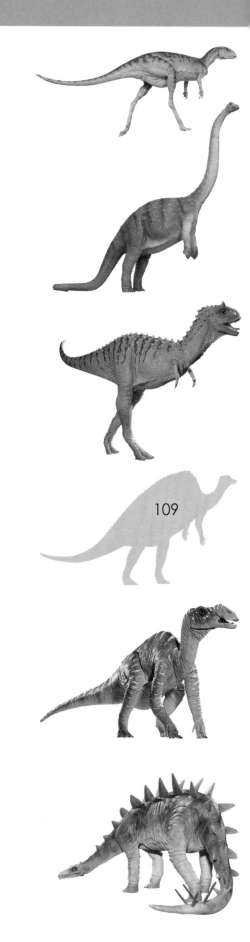

108

109

What do I eat?

Carnivores eat meat and herbivores eat plants.
Circle all of the meat-eating dinosaurs.

I am a Xenotarsosaurus.
I am a carnivore.

I am a Hadrosaurus.
I am a herbivore.

I am a
Riojasaurus.
I am a
herbivore.

I am a
Tyrannosaurus rex.
I am a
carnivore.

I am a Nodosaurus.
I am a herbivore.

I am a Zephyrosaurus.
I am a herbivore.

Drawing dinosaurs

Look at the picture and the dinosaur name, then trace the outlines.

Triceratops

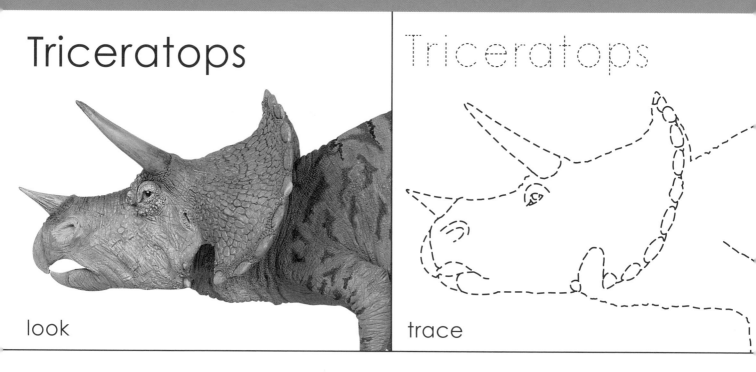

look

Triceratops

trace

Now draw the dinosaur and write its name.

How many?

Count the dinosaurs and write each number in the boxes.

Find the stickers

Find the stickers that fit the spaces below.
Which one matches the picture?

C 112

D 113

110

A

B 111

114

E

Dot to dot

Join the dots to complete the dinosaur pictures, then color them in using the colored dots as a guide.

What's different?

There are six differences between these pictures.
Circle each difference on picture B when you spot them.

A

B

Dinosaur maze

Find a way through the maze so that
the dinosaur can join his friends.

start

finish

Who's missing?

B

Drawing dinosaurs

Look at the picture and the dinosaur name, then trace the outlines.

Stegosaurus

look

Stegosaurus

trace

Now draw the dinosaur and write its name.

S _ _ _ _ _ _ _ _ _ _ _ _

Missing letters

Trace over the letter outlines to complete the words.

tail

horns

teeth

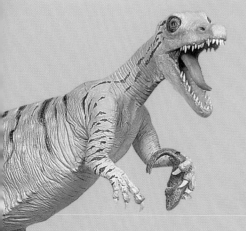

claws

What's different?

There are six differences between these two pictures.
Circle the differences on picture B when you find them.

A

B

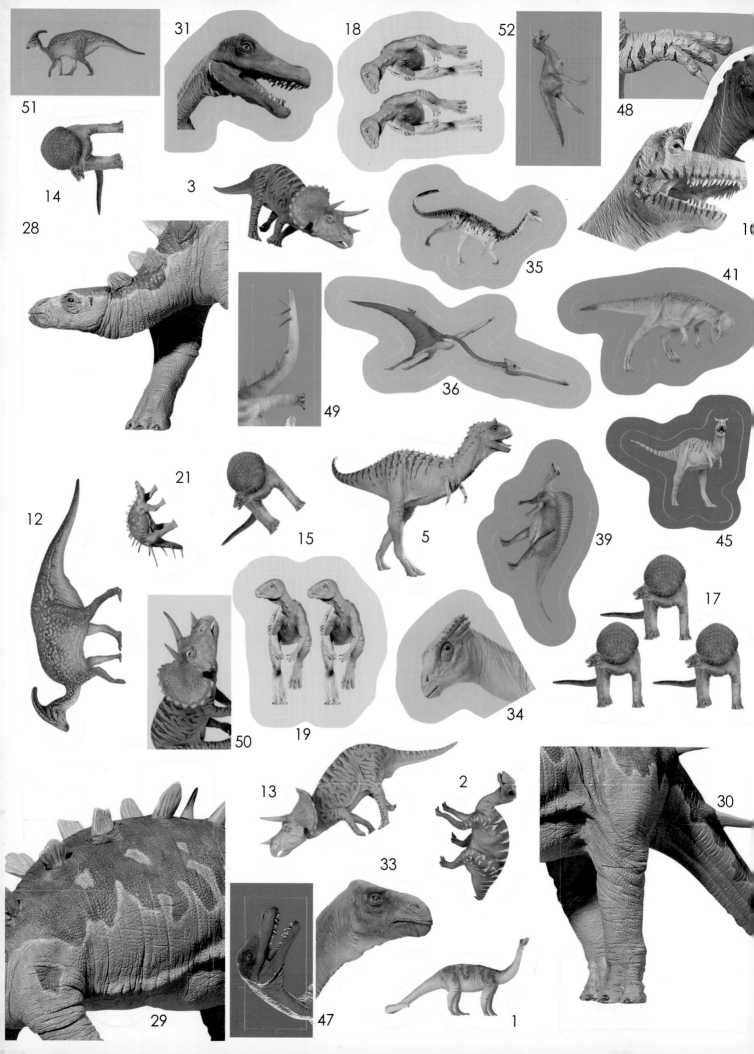

51
31
18
52
48
14
28
3
35
10
41
49
36
21
15
5
39
45
12
50
19
34
17
13
2
33
30
29
47
1

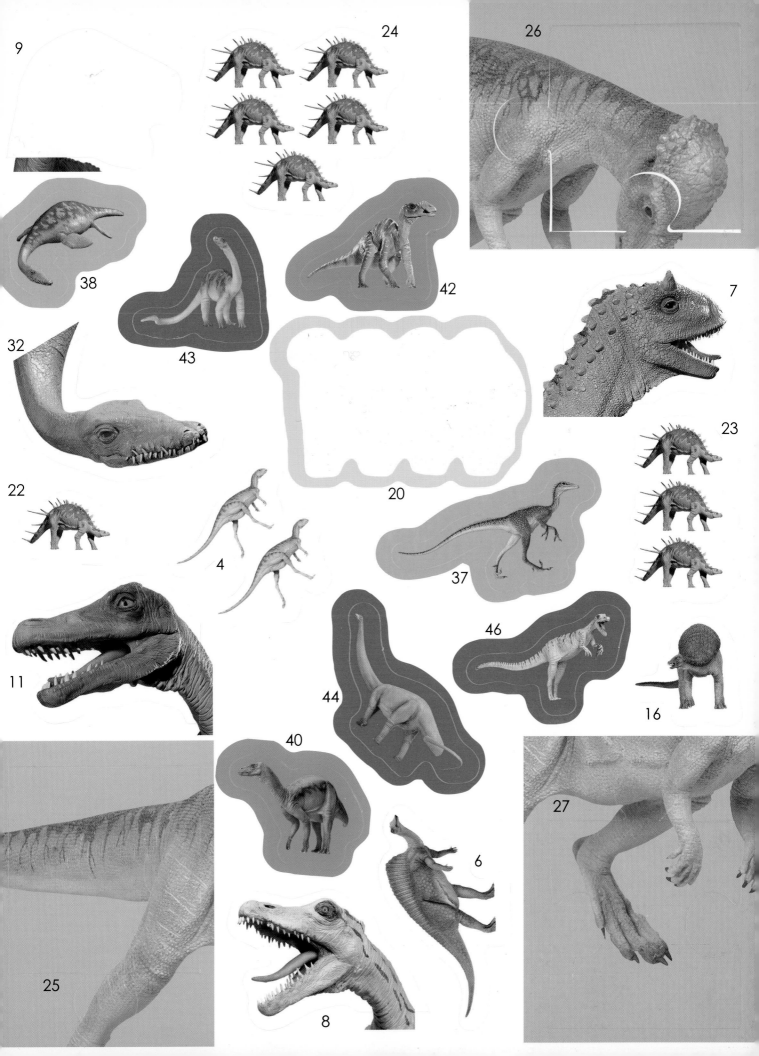

9

24

26

38

32

43

42

7

22

4

20

37

23

11

44

46

16

40

25

6

27

8

Reptile trail

Which trail will take the baby Quetzalcoatlus to its mother?

Matching pairs

Draw lines between the matching pairs of dinosaurs.

Drawing dinosaurs

Look at the picture and dinosaur name, then trace the outlines.

Fabrosaurus

Fabrosaurus

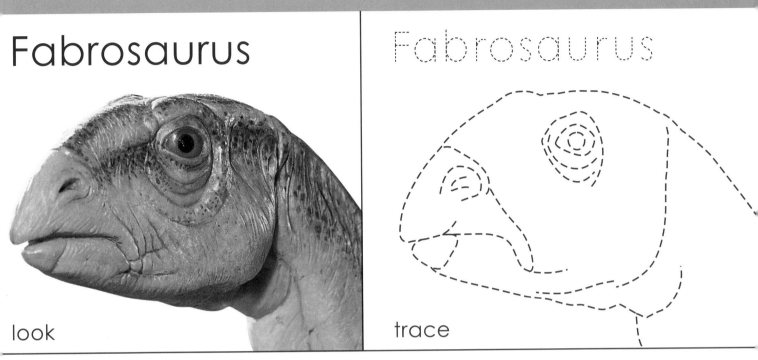

look

trace

Now draw the dinosaur and write its name.

F

Prehistoric picture

Use your pens or pencils to color in this dinosaur scene.

Dinosaur names

Trace over the letters to write these dinosaur names.

Diplodocus

Diplodocus

Ultrasaurus

Ultrasaurus

Janenschia

Janenschia

Drawing dinosaurs

Look at the dinosaur picture and name, then trace the outlines.

Parasaurolophus

Parasaurolophus

look

trace

Now draw the dinosaur and write its name.

P _ _ _ _ _ _ _ _ _ _ _ _ _ _

Macroplata maze

Can you find a way through the maze so the
Macroplata can join his friends?

start

finish

What's different?

Which one of these creatures is different from the others?

Riojasaurus

Quetzalcoatlus

Nodosaurus

Ouranosaurus

Missing halves

Find the stickers, then draw the other halves of the dinosaurs.

Parasaurolophus

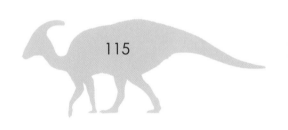

115

116

Triceratops

Adding dinosaurs

Find the stickers, write the numbers of dinosaurs in the boxes, then add them together.

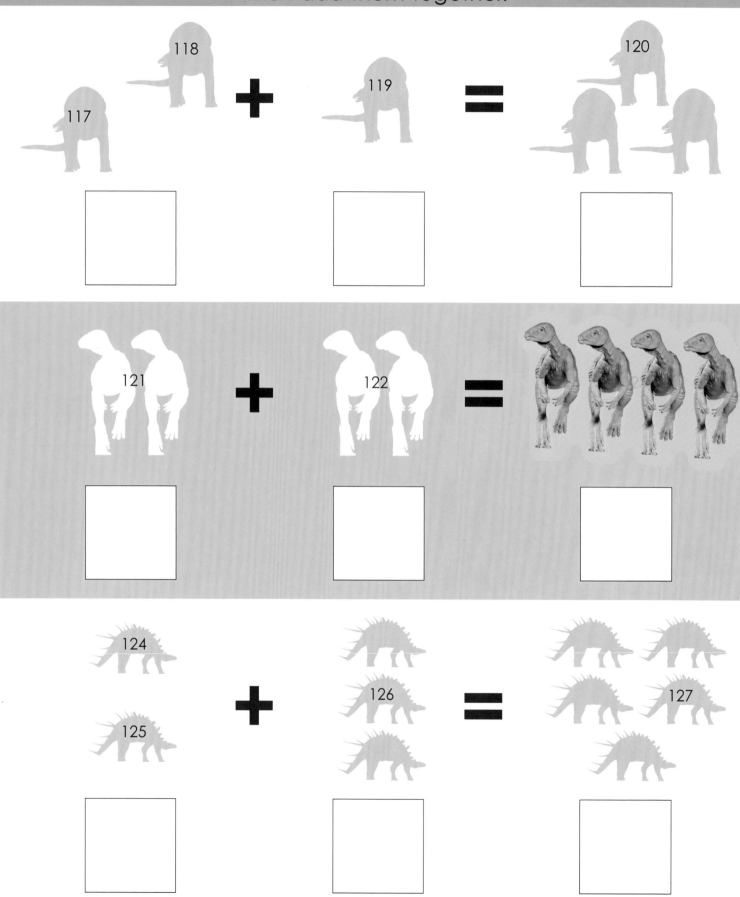

Jigsaw puzzle

Find the jigsaw stickers that complete the pictures.

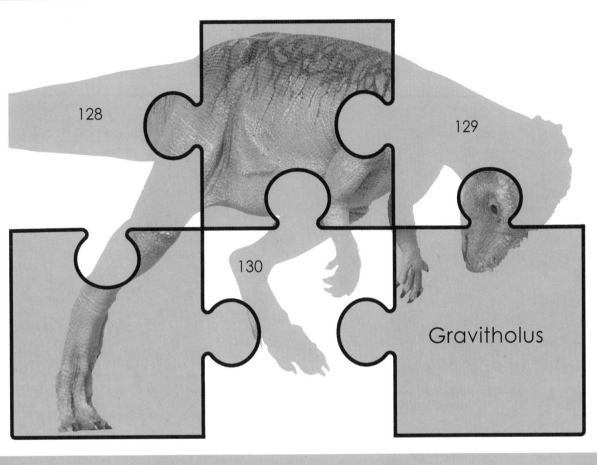

128

129

130

Gravitholus

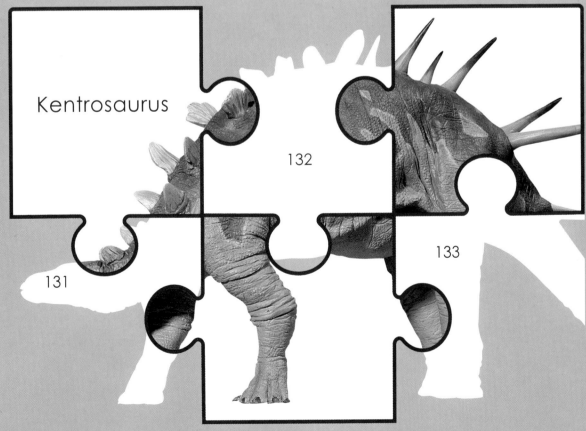

Kentrosaurus

132

131

133

Prehistoric portraits

Find the stickers, then color in the pictures that match.

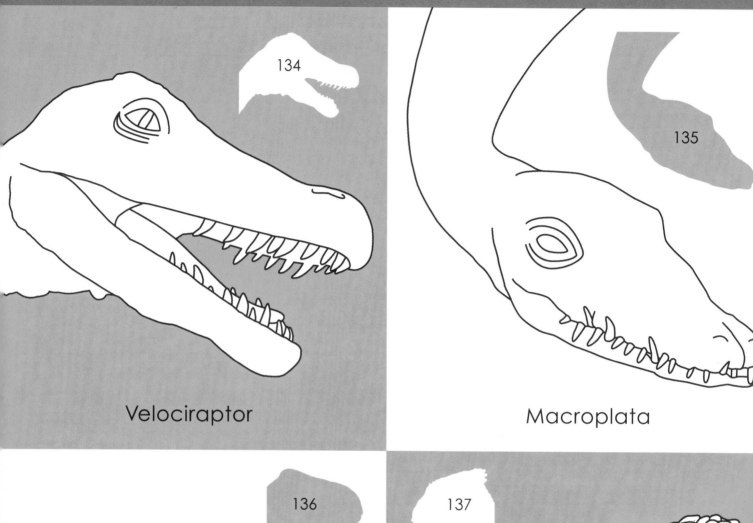

134

135

Velociraptor

Macroplata

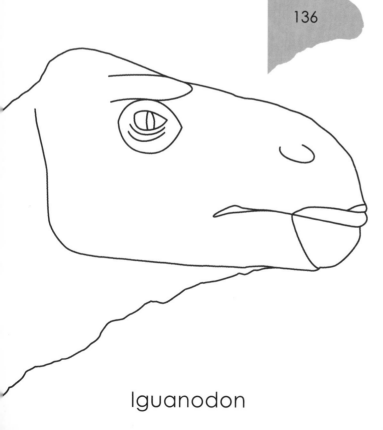

136

Iguanodon

137

Wannanosaurus

Writing practice

Trace over the letters of these dinosaur words.

spikes

eye

neck

tail

Dot to dot

Join the dots to complete the pictures, then color them
in using the colored dots as a guide.

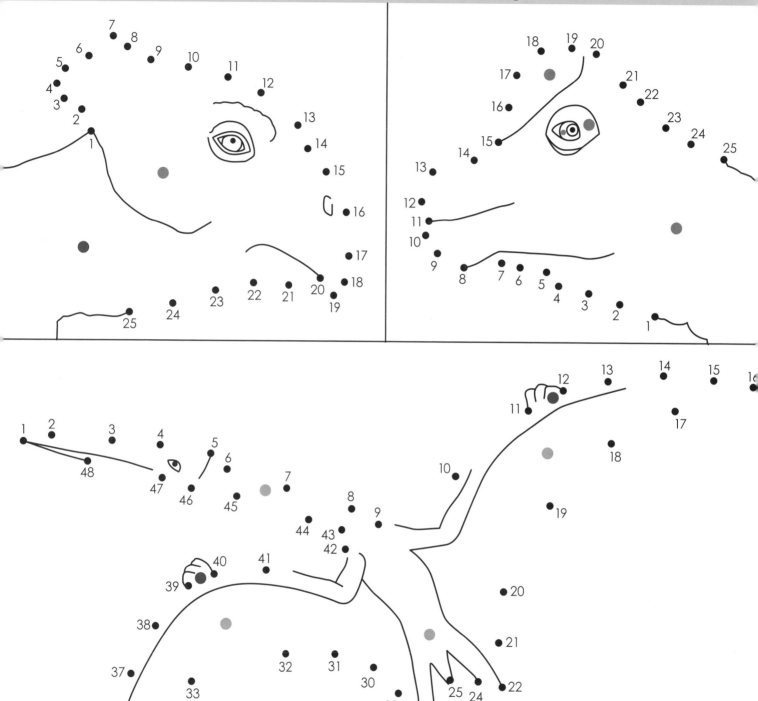

Exactly the same

Only two of these dinosaurs are exactly the same.
Look closely to find them.

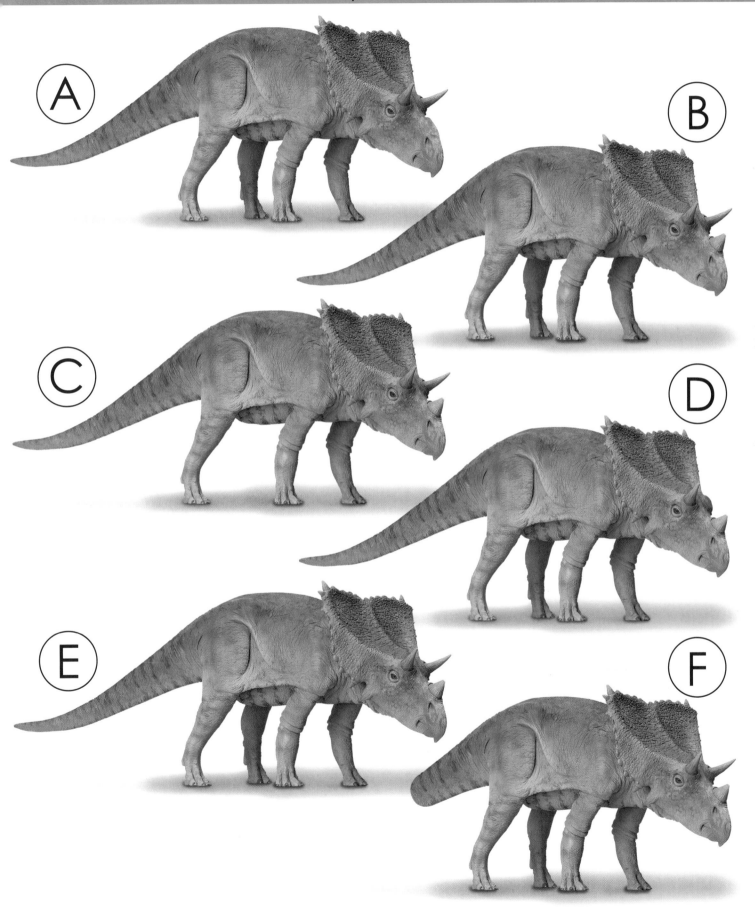

Number practice

Trace over the outlines to practice writing numbers and find the stickers that fit on the opposite page.

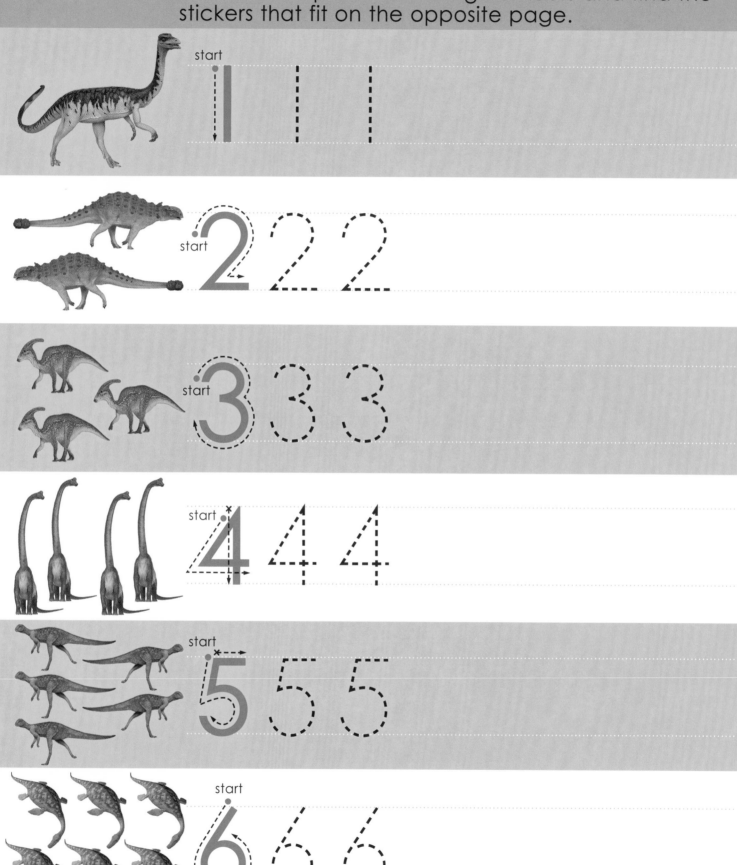

start
1 1 1 1

start
2 2 2 2

start
3 3 3 3

start
4 4 4 4

start
5 5 5 5

start
6 6 6 6

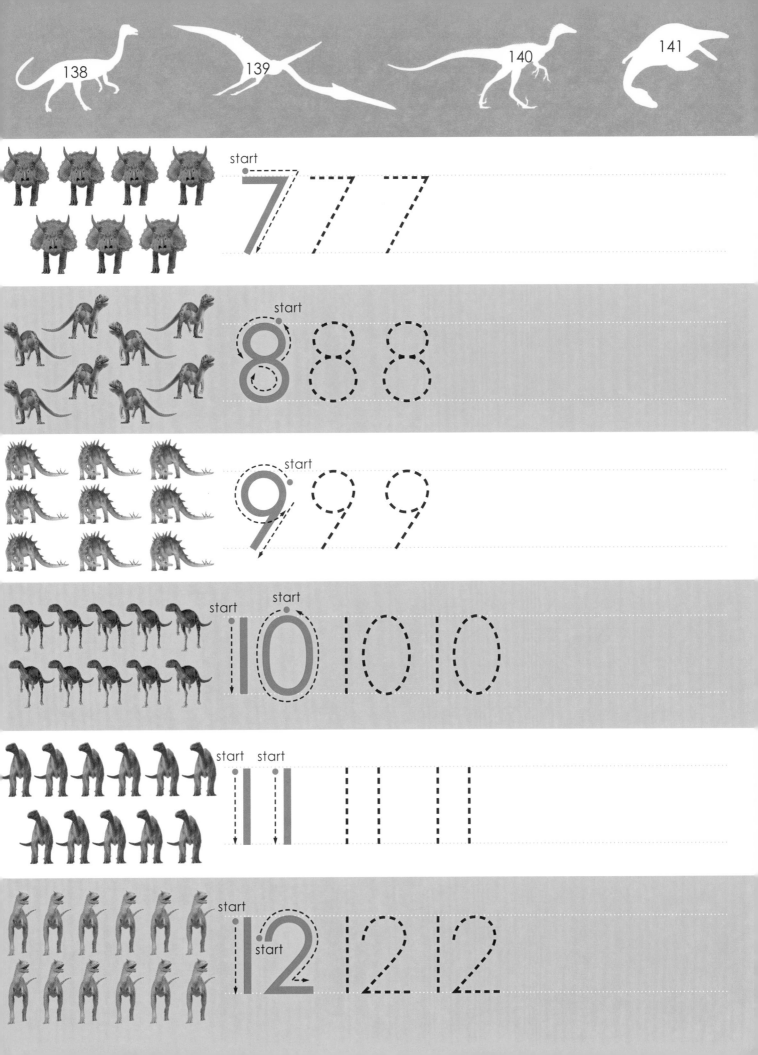

start
7 7 7

start
8 8 8

start
9 9 9

start start
10 10 10

start start
1 1 1 1 1 1

start
start
12 12 12

Letter practice

Trace over the outlines to practice writing letters and find the stickers that fit on the opposite page.

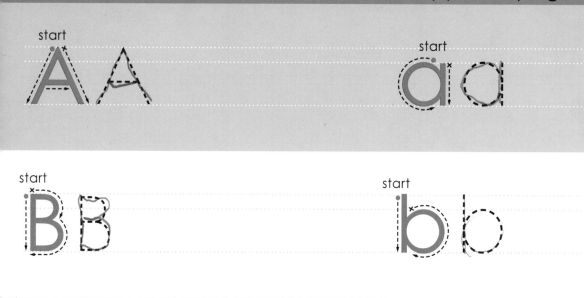

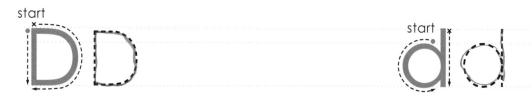

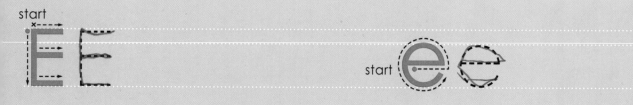

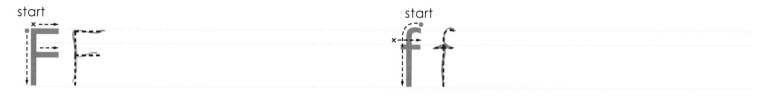

start
G G G

start
g g

start
H H H

start
h h

start
I I

start
i i

start
J J

start
j j

start
K K

start
k k

start
L L

start
l l

Letter practice

Trace over the outlines to practice writing letters and find the stickers that fit on the opposite page.

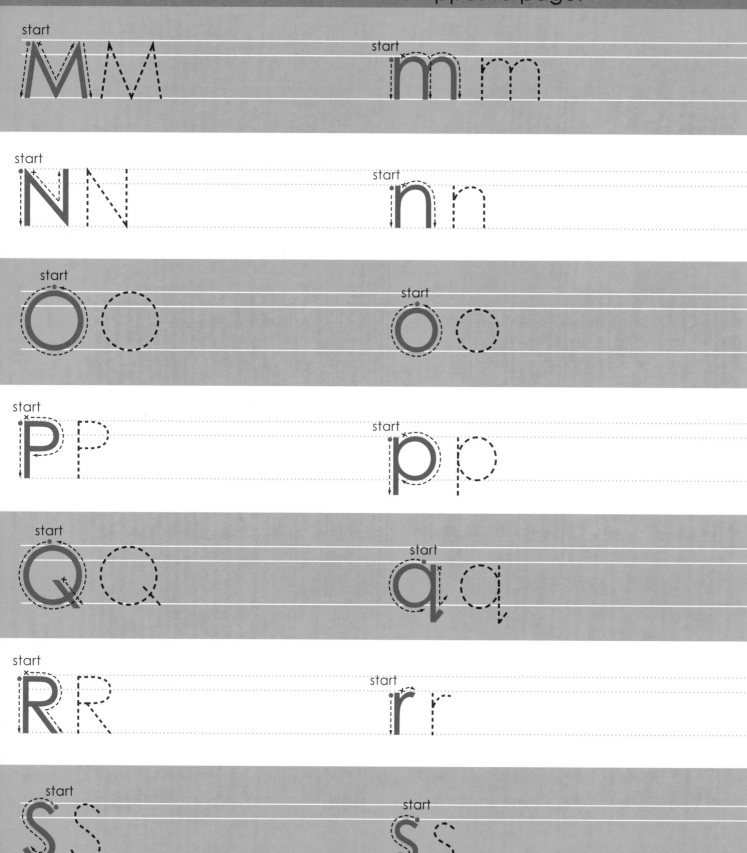

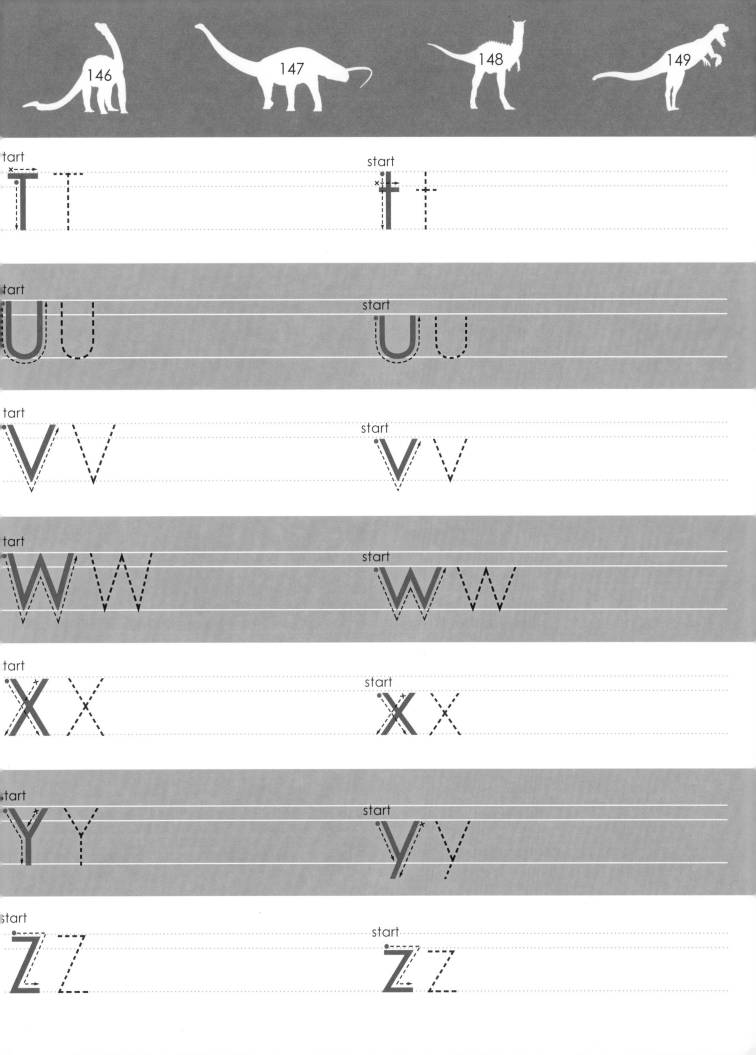

146

147

148

149

start
T T

start
T T

start
U U

start
U U

start
V V

start
V V

start
W W

start
W W

start
X X

start
X X

start
Y Y

start
Y Y

start
Z Z

start
Z Z

Word search

Find the stickers, then look for the words in the box.

x	d	r	y	j	t	e	r	c	o
a	y	i	d	a	a	k	t	l	p
r	e	x	n	e	i	d	i	a	a
e	h	e	a	o	l	e	z	w	s
f	w	o	i	o	s	x	s	s	w
j	i	u	r	u	e	a	i	g	e
g	a	n	h	n	m	t	u	i	t
s	a	e	x	s	s	r	v	r	r
t	e	e	t	h	u	e	n	o	e
b	c	z	s	l	i	s	a	m	x

 150 teeth

 151 claws

 152 tail

 153 horns

 154 dinosaur

 155 T rex